GRAND PRIX
HEROES

GRAND PRIX HEROES

William Ensor

Bath · New York · Singapore · Hong Kong · Cologne · Delhi · Melbourne

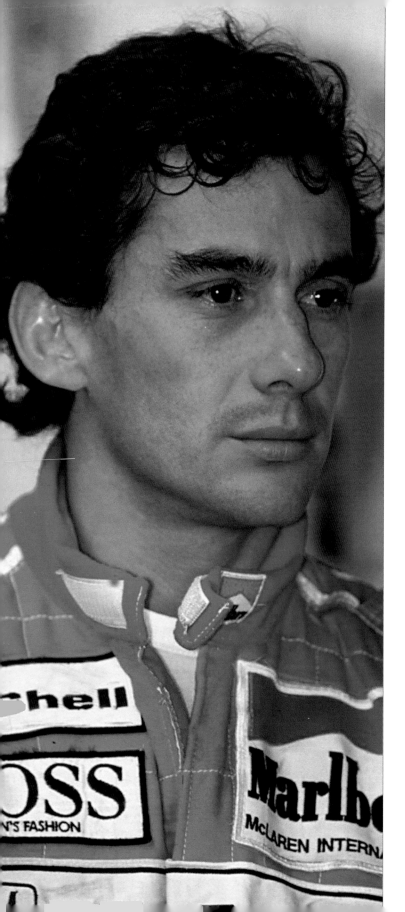

This edition published by Parragon in 2009

Parragon
Queen Street House
4 Queen Street
Bath, BA1 1HE

Text © Parragon Books Ltd 2005
Photographs © LAT
Produced by Atlantic Publishing

Cover images:
Front cover main image © Getty Images/ Jon Feingersh
Front cover small image far right © Getty Images
All other cover images © LAT

ISBN 978-1-4075-7432-5

Printed in Indonesia

Contents

Introduction	7	
Jean Alesi	10	
Fernando Alonso	11	
Mario Andretti	12	
René Arnoux	13	
Alberto Ascari	14	
Rubens Barrichello	16	
Gerhard Berger	17	
Robert Benoist	18	
Georges Boillot	20	
Jack Brabham	21	
Tony Brooks	22	
Jenson Button	23	
Rudolf Caracciola	24	
François Cevert	25	
Louis Chiron	26	
Jim Clark	28	
Peter Collins	30	
David Coulthard	31	
Juan Manuel Fangio	32	
Giuseppe Farina	34	
Emerson Fittipaldi	35	
Timo Glock	36	
José Froilán González	37	
Mika Hakkinen	38	

Lewis Hamilton	39	
Mike Hawthorn	40	
Nick Heidfeld	42	
Damon Hill	43	
Graham Hill	44	
Phil Hill	46	
Denny Hulme	47	
James Hunt	48	
Jacky Ickx	49	
Eddie Irvine	50	
Alan Jones	51	
Heikki Kovaleinen	52	
Robert Kubica	53	
Niki Lauda	54	
Nigel Mansell	55	
Felipe Massa	56	
Bruce McLaren	57	
Guy Moll	58	
Juan Pablo Montoya	59	
Stirling Moss	60	
Felice Nazzaro	62	
Tazio Nuvolari	63	
Olivier Panis	64	
Riccardo Patrese	65	
Ronnie Peterson	66	
Nelson Piquet	67	

Alain Prost	68	
Didier Pironi	70	
Kimi Räikkönen	71	
Carlos Reutemann	72	
Pedro Rodriguez	73	
Jochen Rindt	74	
Keke Rosberg	75	
Nico Rosberg	76	
Bernd Rosemeyer	77	
Jody Scheckter	78	
Ralf Schumacher	79	
Michael Schumacher	80	
Henry Segrave	82	
Raymond Sommer	83	
Ayrton Senna	84	
Jackie Stewart	86	
John Surtees	88	
Jarno Trulli	89	
Achille Varzi	90	
Sebastian Vettel	91	
Gilles Villeneuve	92	
Jacques Villeneuve	93	
Wolfgang von Trips	94	
Mark Webber	95	
Acknowledgements	96	

Introduction

Grand Prix: the ultimate in modern-day gladiatorial combat; man and machine vying for supremacy in the most glamorous sport on the calendar.

Grand Prix Heroes features all the greatest names in a century of Grand Prix racing, an international cast of sporting lions, men of the stature of Fangio, Moss, Clark, Lauda and Schumacher. For some – including Bruce McLaren and Ayrton Senna – the death or glory alternative was grimly realized. But all tested themselves and their machinery to the limit – and often beyond – in their passion for the sport and the pursuit of victory.

GRAND PRIX HEROES

Jean Alesi

B. 11 JUNE 1964, AVIGNON, FRANCE

GRAND PRIX STARTS: 201

GRAND PRIX VICTORIES: 1

POINTS TOTAL: 242

One solitary victory from 201 F1 starts appears deeply unimpressive; yet when one considers that Jean Alesi suffered 83 retirements and got onto the podium on 32 occasions, it gives a more accurate reflection of his ability over a 13-year career at the top level. The statistics show that when his car went the distance, Alesi finished in the top three one race in four.

Stunning debut

Alesi won the French F3 championship in 1987, and two years later took the European Formula 3000 title for Eddie Jordan's team. Ken Tyrell, a man with a long track record of spotting burgeoning talent, gave him his F1 debut at the 1989 French GP. From 16th on the grid he finished a brilliant 4th. He was also in the points at Monza and Jerez to finish in 9th place overall from just half a season's racing.

A full campaign with Tyrell produced two 2nd places. One of those came at the US GP, where he even had the temerity to pass Senna, albeit briefly. It was enough to attract the attention of Frank Williams. Contracts were drawn up, but in the end Alesi opted to join Ferrari in 1991: with hindsight a disastrous decision.

Alesi spent five years at Maranello, a period in which the team was generally looking up the rankings at McLaren, Benetton – and Williams. There were 16 podiums in that time, and even when he finally crossed the line first, at the 1995 Canadian GP, it still only helped him to 5th in the title race.

Switch with Schumacher

A move to Benetton in 1996 initially looked good; eight podiums helped him to 4th in the championship, just behind Michael Schumacher, who had moved in the opposite direction. He peaked with 3rd in 1997, helped by Schumacher's expulsion, before moving on to Sauber. After one false dawn there, and another with Prost, Alesi briefly renewed his acquaintance with Jordan in 2001 before announcing his retirement from F1.

Fernando Alonso

B. 29 July 1981, Oviedo, Spain	
Grand Prix starts: 123*	
Grand Prix victories: 21*	
Points total: 551*	
World Champion 2005, 2006	
*to end of 2008 season	

The son of an amateur kart racer, Alonso first climbed into the cockpit at the age of three, and went on to compete successfully, firstly in his native Spain, then internationally.

By 2000 he had graduated to F3000 earning 4th place in that year's championship. He made his F1 debut with Minardi the following year at the Australian GP, at the age of 19. No points that season, but the Spaniard's potential was spotted and he signed as test driver for Renault for 2002.

2003 saw Alonso promoted into a race seat and the start of his determined efforts to reach the very top of the tree. He scored his maiden victory in Hungary, taking three more podiums that year to finish with 55 points and 6th place.

By contrast, the early part of 2004 was disappointing with team-mate Jarno Trulli out-racing him. As the season progressed Alonso's performance improved, and he finished the year in fourth place.

First world championship

Teamed with Giancarlo Fisichella in 2005. Alonso's first win of the campaign came in Malaysia, followed by victories in Bahrain and at San Marino. Battling against the improving form of McLaren in the shape of Kimi Räikkönen, he clinched the world title in Brazil, finishing 3rd that day. He added 7 wins, 15 podiums and 133 points to his score-sheet, having led the championship from the second race of the season.

Alonso moved to McLaren in 2007, ceding his crown to Ferrari's Räikkönen in a final-round thriller. He tied for the runner-up spot with rookie team-mate Lewis Hamilton. Relations were strained between the two and it was little surprise when Alonso rejoined Renault at the end of the year. He won back-to-back races in 2008, the inaugural Singapore GP and in Japan, to finish 5th in the championship.

Mario Andretti

B. 28 FEBRUARY 1940, MONTONA, ITALY	
GRAND PRIX STARTS: 128	
GRAND PRIX VICTORIES: 12	
POINTS TOTAL: 180	
WORLD CHAMPION 1978	

Mario Andretti wasn't America's first world champion, but his record makes him the greatest to emerge from that country. Andretti's family emigrated to the US when he was in his mid-teens. Barely a decade later he had won a hat-trick of Indy Car titles. He made his F1 debut at Watkins Glen in 1968 for Lotus, a team still reeling from Clark's death. He took pole first time out in an unfamiliar car. After a few more outings for Lotus in 1969, Andretti appeared for the STP March team, with whom he scored his first points. He finished 3rd at Jarama, but generally the car was uncompetitive.

Success with 'ground-effects'

Andretti joined Ferrari and won first time out, Kyalami, 1971, but he didn't concentrate on F1 full-time until 1975, with Parnelli. After a couple of indifferent seasons the team folded and he returned to Lotus. Colin Chapman unveiled the Lotus 78, the first 'ground-effects' car, which Andretti drove to four victories in 1977. Had the engine not failed on several occasions he would undoubtedly have improved on 3rd place in the championship. He did so spectacularly in 1978, winning six races in the new Lotus 79, which dominated the opposition. He was helped by team-mate Ronnie Peterson, who acted as the perfect foil, following the American home four times.

Title confirmed after Peterson tragedy

When they reached Monza, Lotus had the championship won, though it could have gone to either driver. Peterson was involved in a shunt which injured his legs, and Andretti went on to win yet again. The title was his when the news came through that the Swede had died from complications.

Lotus lost its way over the next two years, and a season with Alfa Romeo produced just three points. After a couple of F1 outings in 1982, including an emotional podium finish with Ferrari at Monza that year, Andretti focused on Indy Cars again, taking yet another title in 1984.

René Arnoux

B. 4 JULY 1948, NEAR GRENOBLE, FRANCE

GRAND PRIX STARTS: 149

GRAND PRIX VICTORIES: 7

POINTS TOTAL: 179

René Arnoux arrived in F1 in 1978 having just won the F2 championship in a works Martini. Both driver and team stepped up in class, but the latter soon folded and Arnoux ended the year driving for Surtees. In 1979 he took a second berth at Renault. The previous year the team had only fielded Jean-Pierre Jabouille, who, ironically, had pipped Arnoux for the F2 title in 1976. In the competitive RS 10 he twice took pole, although his best results were 2nd at Silverstone and Watkins Glen, from 5th and 7th on the grid respectively.

One more victory than champion

Arnoux made the early running in 1980, winning two of the first three races, Interlagos and Kyalami. He couldn't sustain his form and ended the year in 6th, a long way adrift of Jones and Piquet.

There were four more poles in 1981 but he failed to convert his undoubted speed into wins; 2nd in Austria was the highlight of a thin year. He won twice in 1982, one more victory than champion Rosberg, though with the best eleven scores counting the Frenchman didn't have enough to back it up and finished 6th. His win at Paul Ricard didn't endear him to team-mate Prost or the bosses as he breached team orders. It was to be his last campaign with Renault.

Best season at Maranello

1983 was the closest Arnoux came to striking gold. Now with Ferrari, he won three GPs but his failure to score in the last two rounds left him 3rd in the championship. It was downhill at Maranello thereafter: a couple of 2nd places in 1984; then, after finishing 4th in Brazil, the opening round of the 1985 championship, he was fired. He returned the following year with Ligier, where he spent the final four years of his F1 career. The first of those was the most productive: no podiums but 14 points put him 8th in the championship. The final three campaigns yielded a total of just three points.

Alberto Ascari

B. 13 JULY 1918, MILAN, ITALY
D. 26 MAY 1955
GRAND PRIX STARTS: 31
GRAND PRIX VICTORIES: 13
POINTS TOTAL: 140.64
WORLD CHAMPION 1952, 1953

As well as being legendary names in the world of motor sport, Alberto Ascari and his father Antonio had careers that followed an eerily similar path. Ascari Sr, one of the premier drivers of the post-WWI era, was killed while competing at the 1925 French GP. He was 36 and left behind a wife and two children, one of whom was seven-year-old Alberto. Thirty years later Alberto — also married with two children — lost his life on the track at the age of 36.

Ascari began his racing career on two wheels before turning to cars in 1940. That was in the famous Mille Miglia road race, driving for Ferrari. Team boss Enzo Ferrari had been a contemporary of Ascari's father; a generation on, Ascari Jr and Maranello were about to make a huge impact on Formula One.

Villoresi's protégé

Ascari made his Grand Prix debut in 1947, winning several races over the next three years. At the 1948 British GP he and his Maserati team-mate and mentor, Luigi Villoresi, had to start from the back of the grid after arriving late. They carved their way through the field to finish 1st and 2nd, and although Villoresi took top honours, he marked out his protégé to go to the very top of the sport.

By the end of the following season, when he won the Swiss and Italian GPs, Ascari was back in the Ferrari fold. He finished 5th in the inaugural world championship of 1950, a series dominated by Alfa Romeo. A year later he won in Germany and Italy but it wasn't quite enough to wrest the title from Fangio and Alfa. The next two seasons saw Ascari at the height of his powers. He missed the 1952 curtain-raiser in Switzerland to try his luck in the Indy 500, but was back in time for Spa, winning not only that race but the next five too. With only the four best finishes counting, it meant that Ascari was able to discard two victories and still claim the world crown.

Nine wins in a row

Ascari's victory at Spa on 21 June 1953 completed a run of nine successive wins in a twelve-month period. He retained his title with a win at Bremgarten, the penultimate round of the 1953 championship.

Ascari signed for Lancia to drive the new D50 in 1954, but the car wasn't ready until the final race, the Spanish GP. He put it on pole first time out but a clutch failure ended a miserable championship series. 1955 began promisingly, despite Ascari putting the D50 into the harbour when running strongly at Monaco. He walked away unscathed, only to be killed four days later while testing a Ferrari sports car at Monza. He remains the last Italian to win the world championship.

Rubens Barrichello

B. 23 MAY 1972, SÃO PAULO, BRAZIL

GRAND PRIX STARTS: 271*

GRAND PRIX VICTORIES: 9*

POINTS TOTAL: 530*

*TO END OF 2008 SEASON

Runner-up to Schumacher in the championship in 2002 and 2004, Barrichello has shown on numerous occasions that he has the talent to beat anyone on his day.

Pips Coulthard to F3 title

Barrichello went to Europe after winning five national kart titles in his teens. He immediately won the GM Lotus Euro-series, then beat Coulthard to the 1991 British F3 title, driving for West Surrey Racing. He made his F1 debut for Jordan in 1993. In only his third race, the European GP at Donington, he was running 2nd before retiring, while his first points came at Suzuka, where he finished 5th.

He began 1994 strongly, including a podium finish at the Pacific GP, but suffered a big spill during practice at Imola. Deeply affected by Senna's death, he showed great fortitude in taking a brilliant pole at Spa. He was 6th that year, and having failed to improve on that in the next two seasons, left to join the Stewart team in 1997.

Replaces Irvine at Maranello

Finishing second to Schumacher at Monaco was that year's highlight. After a disappointing 1998, his loyalty to Stewart was rewarded with three podiums and seventh in the 1999 championship, though it was team-mate Johnny Herbert who gave the team its first victory. In 2000 he replaced Irvine as Ferrari no. 2, scoring his maiden win from 18th on the grid at a wet Hockenheim.

New challenge with Honda

After six years as Ferrari's No.2, 33-year-old Barrichello took up a fresh challenge with Honda. The next three seasons yielded just 41 points, though the 2008 Turkish GP, his 257th, did see him pass Riccardo Patrese's record for F1 starts. Honda's decision to withdraw at the end of 2008 left 36-year-old Barrichello's future in doubt. but he went into the 2009 season, his 17th in F1, driving for the new Brawn GP team.

Gerhard Berger

B. 27 AUGUST 1959, WORGL, AUSTRIA

GRAND PRIX STARTS: 210

GRAND PRIX VICTORIES: 10

POINTS TOTAL: 386

Gerhard Berger is one of only a handful of drivers to compete in over 200 F1 races, a consistent performer in his 14-year career at the top level. He made his debut at the 1984 Austrian GP for ATS, finishing 6th in only his second race. A move to Arrows yielded three points in 1985, but his career then took off. He joined Benetton, which had just evolved from Toleman, scoring both his and the team's maiden victory in Mexico.

Answers Maranello call

Ferrari came calling, and Berger embarked on the first of two stints at Maranello. He won the final two races to secure 5th place in 1987;

only the 'big four' – Prost, Senna, Piquet and Mansell – finished ahead of him. A year later only the runaway McLarens of Senna and Prost got the better of him, and his one victory came in the best place of all for a Ferrari man, Monza. New team-mate Mansell outscored him in 1989, though in an indifferent season he enjoyed a huge slice of luck: escaping a big accident at Imola with minor injuries.

In Senna's shadow

Three years at McLaren followed, a period where he was naturally in Senna's shadow. He was a regular on the podium, but scored just three wins. At Suzuka in 1991 Senna moved over on the last lap to let him taste victory. And in Montreal a year later he inherited the lead after Senna retired with electrical trouble.

Berger returned to Ferrari in 1993, a period when Maranello was playing second fiddle to Williams and Benetton. He did win at Hockenheim in 1994 to break Ferrari's longest winless streak, a season in which he finished 3rd yet again, a position he would never improve upon.

His final two campaigns were back at Benetton. With team bosses hinting that his days were numbered, Berger announced his retirement before Hockenheim, then won the race in brilliant style again.

Robert Benoist

B. 20 MARCH 1895, RAMBOUILLET, FRANCE

D. 9 SEPTEMBER 1944

Robert Benoist was a fighter ace during WWI, starting his racing career when hostilities ended. He became Delage's works driver in 1924, beginning a four-year spell that would secure his place in motor sport's hall of fame.

In 1925 he teamed up with Albert Divo to win the French GP, the race which claimed the life of Antonio Ascari. The following year Benoist was leading the inaugural British GP at Brooklands, despite stopping to effect repairs. The design of the Delage meant that the exhaust ran under the floor pan, burning the driver's feet. The low-tech solution to the problem involved having a tray of cold water on hand, and eventually Benoist succumbed. The less experienced and less gifted M. Dubonnet finished the race in 3rd place.

Awarded Légion d'Honneur

A year later the car was much improved, modifications including the rerouting of the exhaust system. It was to be Benoist's golden year, in which he won four of the five premier GPs. He won in Italy by over 20 minutes and after successes in the French and Spanish GPs he returned to Brooklands for the 1 October race. It was a clean sweep for Delage, Benoist crossing the line ahead of Boulier and Divo. He beat the previous year's winning time by nearly twelve minutes, even though the drivers this year had to complete 15 more laps of the 2.6-mile circuit. His average speed of 85.59 mph was only just outside the fastest lap set by Segrave in 1926. Benoist's extraordinary achievement that year earned him the Légion d'Honneur.

Captured while working for SOE

He joined Bugatti when Delage withdrew, and even came back from a five-year semi-retirement to score some notable victories, including Le Mans 1937, a victory shared with Wimille. He retired for good that year.

Benoist worked for the Special Operations Executive during WWII. He escaped the clutches of the Gestapo in dramatic fashion in 1943 but was recaptured the following year and executed at Buchenwald concentration camp.

Georges Boillot

B. 3 AUGUST 1884

D. 21 APRIL 1916

The quixotic Georges Boillot became a French legend for his efforts in three successive French Grands Prix. He won in 1912 and 1913, and although he failed to complete the hat-trick at Lyon in 1914, it was such an heroic effort that his reputation was, if anything, enhanced.

Victory in Bugatti-designed car

Boillot, an engineer by training, began his racing career in 1906. He was part of a team that built its own car to run under the Peugeot banner. The partnership made its competitive debut in 1909, and three years later, Boillot won his first French GP, at Dieppe. That day he drove an L76 model, designed by the young Ettore Bugatti, the first car to feature four valves per cylinder.

In 1913 Boillot won the Coupe de l'Auto, then defended his French GP title with a victory at Amiens. This time he ran a Peugeot EX3, covering the 916.98 km in 7 hr. 56 min. 22.4 sec. and finishing over three minutes ahead of Jules Goux.

'Race of the century'

In 1914 he set a new speed record of 99.86 mph, just failing to break the magical three-figure barrier, and would have won the Indy 500 but for tyre trouble. The French GP that year turned out to be his final competitive appearance. It was dubbed 'the race of the century', both because it was the most exciting ever seen, and for the fact that as this was the only Grand Prix on the European calendar, it was a de facto winner-take-all world championship. It attracted a 37-strong field from 13 manufacturers.

Tears as Peugeot disintegrates

Boillot was favourite to complete the 20 laps of the 37.63-km circuit first in the new L45. It turned into a race between Peugeot and Mercedes, France v Germany, who were about to find themselves on opposite sides of a global conflict. On lap 18 Mercedes' Christian Lautenschlager passed Boillot's disintegrating Peugeot, and a tearful Frenchman retired on the last circuit.

Boillot swapped one cockpit for another, becoming a fighter pilot in WWI. He was killed in a dogfight over Verdun, after single-handedly taking on several German planes.

Jack Brabham

B. 2 APRIL 1926, HURSTVILLE, AUSTRALIA

GRAND PRIX STARTS: 126

GRAND PRIX VICTORIES: 14

POINTS TOTAL: 261

WORLD CHAMPION 1959, 1960, 1966

Jack Brabham learned his trade on the dirt-track circuits of his native Australia before arriving in Britain in 1955 to test himself against the cream of Europe. He immediately gravitated towards the Cooper stable, and between them they changed the face of the sport in the late 1950s. 'Black Jack' and John Cooper were the visionaries behind the rear-engined revolution which produced a first GP win in 1958. Stirling Moss had that honour, driving a Rob Walker Cooper. Brabham gave the works team its first success at Monaco in 1959, and also won at Aintree to set up a championship showdown at Sebring in December. He ran out of fuel on the final lap and pushed his car across the line in 4th place — only to find that Moss's retirement meant that his efforts had been unnecessary.

Sets up own team

In 1960 Brabham reeled off five wins to retain his title with two rounds to spare. He slipped down the rankings in 1961, Cooper struggling to adapt to the new 1.5-litre formula. Brabham then set up his own team, and before the 1962 season was out had become the first man to notch championship points in his own car.

Team boss and champion

It was Dan Gurney who gave the fledgling team its first victory, in the 1964 French GP. In the same race two years later Jack matched that achievement, and he followed it up with three more victories in 1966, to win his third world championship. He remains the only man to lift the crown in a car bearing his name.

Brabham competed for four more years, claiming his 14th and final victory at Kyalami in 1970, a month short of his 44th birthday. He called it a day after finishing 5th in that year's championship, and sold the team to Bernie Ecclestone the following year.

Tony Brooks

B. 25 FEBRUARY 1932, DUKINFIELD, ENGLAND

GRAND PRIX STARTS: 38

GRAND PRIX VICTORIES: 6 (1 SHARED)

POINTS TOTAL: 75

Tony Brooks gave up a career in dentistry to concentrate on motor racing. In the late 1950s he, like Stirling Moss, came close to winning the coveted world crown, having been tipped by no less a figure than Fangio to take over the mantle as Grand Prix racing's foremost driver.

1955 was Brooks's breakthrough year. He moved to single-seaters, winning the non-championship Syracuse GP in a Connaught on his Formula One debut. The following year saw him contest his first world championship, with BRM. It was to prove a false dawn as Brooks was thrown from his car during practice at Silverstone, and spent the remainder of the year competing in sports-car events.

Shared victory with Moss

Brooks then signed for Vanwall, where he finished 5th and 3rd in the next two championship campaigns. The 1957 British GP gave him his first taste of victory, albeit shared with team-mate Stirling Moss, who took over his car mid-distance. In 1958 Brooks won three times – in Belgium, Germany and Italy – but a succession of retirements hampered his chance of lifting the crown and he had to settle for 3rd place, behind Hawthorn and Moss.

Runner-up to Brabham

Vanwall withdrew at the end of the year and Brooks moved to Ferrari. There were two more victories but it wasn't quite enough to outdo the formidable combination of Jack Brabham and the revolutionary rear-engined Cooper. Brooks finished the season runner-up, four points adrift of the Australian.

In his final two seasons Brooks slipped down the rankings, garnering a total of just 13 points. In 1960 he drove an uncompetitive Cooper T51 for the Yeoman Credit team, then rejoined BRM for his swansong campaign. There were flashes of his great prowess but the hardware at his disposal was never going to make a dramatic impact. Recently married, Brooks retired at the end of 1961 to concentrate on his garage business.

Jenson Button

B. 19 JANUARY 1980, FROME, ENGLAND

GRAND PRIX STARTS: 155*

GRAND PRIX VICTORIES: 1*

POINTS TOTAL: 232*

* TO END OF 2008 SEASON

Button was something of a prodigy, having starred in Cadet Karts at the age of eight. He won the British championship in 1990 and 1991, going on to finish runner-up in the world championship in 1995. Two years later the 17-year-old became the youngest winner of the European Super A championship, and was seen as one of motor sport's rising stars.

Young Driver of the Year

In 1998 he continued his upward surge, taking the British Formula Ford title and picking up the prestigious McLaren-Autosport Young Driver of the Year award.

Next it was on to the F3 championship, where he topped the podium three times and finished 3rd against much more experienced opposition. His performances earned him a test with McLaren and Prost in late 1999, but it was Williams who got his signature. Button finished 6th in only his second GP, Interlagos 2000, becoming the youngest Briton to notch a championship point.

Button challenges Ferrari dominance

Button spent the next two seasons with Benetton-Renault. In 2002 he scored in seven races and finished 7th in the final table. He moved to BAR in 2003, regularly outperforming team-mate Jacques Villeneuve, a former world champion. In 2004 only the Ferraris got the better of Button, who stood on the podium ten times and scored 85 points.

Button started 2005 poorly, with a disqualification at the San Marino GP, and hence a three-race ban. His performance improved with 3rd places at both Hockenheim and Spa-Francorchamps, ending the season with 37 points and 9th place overall. A number of contractual controversies during 2004 and 2005 between Button, Honda and Williams, led to speculation that he would be leaving BAR. In fact he remained with the Honda team during 2005 and went on to win his first race with them at the Hungaroring in 2006. Button notched just nine points over the next two seasons, and and went into the 2009 campaign under the new Brawn GP banner.

Rudolf Caracciola

B. 30 JANUARY 1901, REMAGEN, GERMANY

D. 28 SEPTEMBER 1959

No less a figure than Alfred Neubauer believed that Rudi Caracciola was the greatest driver of them all. Neubauer was the man behind Mercedes' racing division for over 20 years, an era which encompassed the triumphs of Nuvolari and Rosemeyer, and the world championship successes of Fangio and Ascari.

The 'Regenmeister'

Caracciola was a Mercedes employee when he took up racing in 1922. Four years later, he convinced his bosses to allow him to enter a factory car in the inaugural German GP at Avus. It began disastrously, Caracciola stalling on the grid and starting from the back of the 44-strong field. He carved his way through the pack in appalling conditions, showing the kind of skill which would earn him

the sobriquet 'Regenmeister' – Rainmaster – long before it was applied to Michael Schumacher. He even fixed a misfire problem – drivers then had to carry out their own repairs – before returning to the track to win the race in front of 500,000 delirious fans.

Hat-trick of European titles

In 1931 Caracciola became the first non-Italian to win the Mille Miglia, an achievement that was unequalled until Stirling Moss's victory in 1955. An accident at the 1933 Monaco GP left him with a permanent limp, yet his greatest days were still ahead. From 1934, when Mercedes returned to GP racing, through to WWII Caracciola was the marque's no. 1 driver. He won the German GP five times and the Eifelrennen on four occasions, results which helped him to become European champion – the pre-1950 equivalent of world's best – three times between 1935 and 1938. The year he didn't win the championship – 1936 – it went to arch-rival Rosemeyer. The competitive friction between the two extended to world record attempts. It was while trying to recapture the record from Caracciola that Rosemeyer was killed in 1938. Another major accident and worsening health hampered his post-war efforts on the track. He contracted bone disease and died in 1959, aged 58.

François Cevert

B. 25 FEBRUARY 1944, PARIS CITY, MEXICO

D. 6 OCTOBER 1973

GRAND PRIX STARTS: 47

GRAND PRIX VICTORIES: 1

POINTS TOTAL: 89

François Cevert chose a career as a racing driver instead of concert pianist, harbouring an ambition to become France's first world champion. He won the country's F3 title in 1968, driving his own Tecno, and was given a works F2 drive the following year. That season also saw him make his F1 debut, in Tecno's F2 car at the Nurburgring. He qualified 4th but lasted just nine laps.

Snapped up by Tyrell

Cevert began 1970 still in F2, but when Johnny Servoz-Gavin quit the sport after just three rounds, he was signed to partner Jackie Stewart at Tyrell. Sixth place at Monza was his best result that year, but Tyrell was a team in transition. It ran a March chassis, awaiting the development of its own, which was ready in time for the start of the 1971 campaign. Cevert finished 2nd in France and Germany, then at Watkins Glen, with the title already in Stewart's hands, he scored his maiden victory. He ended the year in 3rd place in the championship.

Lotus, McLaren and Ferrari were all stronger in 1972. There were two more 2nd places for the Frenchman, behind the Lotus of champion-in-waiting Fittipaldi at the Belgian GP, and Stewart in the season's final race, Watkins Glen. He finished 6th overall.

Poised to take over Stewart mantle

Tyrell roared back in 1973. Stewart held off the Lotus challenge of Fittipaldi and Peterson to claim his third world crown, while Cevert gave brilliant support. There were no wins but he crossed the line in 2nd place on six occasions. Stewart already had the title sewn up before Watkins Glen, the final round. He planned to retire after what would have been his hundredth Grand Prix, leaving Cevert poised to take over as the team's no. 1. But the Frenchman's fatal accident during qualifying brought Stewart's decision forward, and Tyrell withdrew as a mark of respect. Cevert ended the year in posthumous 4th place in the championship.

Louis Chiron

B. 3 AUGUST 1899, MONTE CARLO, MONACO

D. 22 JUNE 1979

The 1930s was Louis Chiron's heyday yet he was such a wily campaigner – his nickname was le Vieux Renard, the Old Fox – that he was still competing at the top level in the early years of the world championship, by which time he was over 50. He got on to the podium in his home GP of 1950, finishing third behind Fangio and Ascari in his Maserati. Five years later, when he was three months short of his 56th birthday, he scored a point for 6th place at Monaco, a record it is difficult to envisage being beaten.

Chauffeur to Foch and Pétain

If Chiron was capable of impressive performances in his later years, he was equally outstanding in his youth. He was still in his teens when he was given the responsibility of being chauffeur to Marshals Foch and Pétain during WWI. By 1923 he had acquired a Bugatti, and was that marque's top driver in the late 1920s and early 1930s, before moving to Alfa Romeo. His victory at the 1934 French GP was the last success for the famous Tipo P3, the first true monoposto racing car.

Five-time French GP winner

Chiron won just about all the major races of the day. He was a five-time winner of the French GP, his last victory coming in 1949, when he was almost 50. He won the Spanish and Czech GPs, each on three occasions, and also enjoyed victories in Germany, Italy and Belgium. In 1933 Chiron won at Le Mans, a victory shared with Luigi Chinetti.

A noted socialite and ladies' man as well as a top racing driver, Chiron was instrumental in bringing Grand Prix racing to his native principality. When his racing days were over he continued to play an active organizational role in the most glamorous race on the calendar. Monaco's most famous son was honoured with the erection of a statue on the course and also had one of the famous curves named after him.

Jim Clark

B. 4 MARCH 1936, KILMANY, SCOTLAND

D. 7 APRIL 1968

GRAND PRIX STARTS: 72

GRAND PRIX VICTORIES: 25

POINTS TOTAL: 274

WORLD CHAMPION 1963, 1965

If Fangio was the supreme champion of the 1950s, Jim Clark inherited that mantle the following decade. The unassuming sheep farmer from the Borders was scintillatingly quick, famous for his smoothness and effortless control. His brand of speed came from a computer-like brain, not cavalier risk-taking.

Clark spent his entire career at Lotus, which he joined in 1960, forging a formidable partnership with team boss Colin Chapman. His first GP outing came at Zandvoort in 1960. He retired that day, but had picked up a respectable eight points by the end of the season. It was three points more and one place higher the following year, when the Lotus 21 was no match for the Ferraris. The campaign was overshadowed by Clark's involvement in the crash at Monza in which 14 spectators were killed and Ferrari's Wolfgang von Trips lost his life.

Lotus failure costs Clark title

Clark's maiden victory came at the 1962 Belgian GP. Two more wins that season put him in contention for the championship going into the final round, in South Africa. He was heading for the victory which would have snatched the crown from Graham Hill when his Lotus failed.

Clark brushed aside that disappointment to take the championship the following year, winning seven of the ten rounds. With only six scores counting, he had the luxury of being able to discard one of his victories. Problems with the new Lotus 33 hampered his performances in 1964, yet he still went into the final race, the Mexican GP, with a chance of retaining his title. Clark led for 63 of the 65 laps before the car again gave out.

Second maximum points haul

Clark stormed to his second world crown in 1965 with another maximum haul from the six races where he reached the line. Victory in the Indy 500 made it a notable double.

1966 was a relatively lean season, Lotus struggling to adapt to the new 3-litre formula, but early in 1967 the new Cosworth DFV engine arrived and Clark was immediately back on song. Four more wins put him 3rd in the championship behind the two powerful Brabhams.

Clark opened his 1968 account with a victory at Kyalami. It was his 25th career success, putting him one ahead of Fangio in the all-time list. He was still only 31 and at the height of his powers. With the second championship race not due until May, Clark competed in a F2 race at Hockenheim on 7 April. His car left the track and hit a tree, killing him instantly.

Peter Collins

B. 6 NOVEMBER 1931, KIDDERMINSTER, ENGLAND
D. 3 AUGUST 1958
GRAND PRIX STARTS: 32
GRAND PRIX VICTORIES: 3
POINTS TOTAL: 47

Peter Collins graduated to Formula One as a 20-year-old, making his championship debut with HWM at the 1952 Swiss GP. He struggled to make any impression in what was an unreliable car, a pattern that was to be repeated over the next three years. In that time he drove for Vanwall and BRM as well as HWM, but his main successes came in sports cars with Aston Martin's works team.

When the hardware allowed, Collins was certainly quick, a fact not lost on Ferrari, who signed him for 1956. He played the supporting role to Fangio, notably at Monaco, where he handed his Lancia-Ferrari over after the three-time champion's car failed. Back-to-back victories at Spa and Reims showed that Collins was a serious contender in his own right.

Sacrifices title hopes

Both Collins and Jean Behra went into the final race, Monza, knowing they could snatch the title from Fangio with a victory and fastest lap, provided the Argentine failed to score. With Behra and Fangio out of the race, Collins allowed Fangio to take over his car, sacrificing his own championship ambitions. Fangio duly took the title, while Moss won the race relegating Collins to 3rd in the final table.

1957 was something of an anticlimax, Collins recording just two 3rd places in a season dominated by Fangio and Maserati.

Fatal crash at Nurburgring

1958 augured well as Ferrari fielded the new 246 Dino. Collins registered two top-six finishes before beating team-mate Mike Hawthorn into 2nd place at Silverstone. Collins lay 3rd in the championship as the circus moved to the Nurburgring. There, vying for the lead with Tony Brooks' Vanwall, Collins crashed and was fatally injured when he was flung from his car. He was 26. Collins finished a posthumous 5th in that year's championship, but it was for his magnanimous act of sportsmanship in helping Fangio claim his fourth world crown that he is best remembered.

David Coulthard

B. 27 MARCH 1971, TWYNHOLM, SCOTLAND

GRAND PRIX STARTS: 247

GRAND PRIX VICTORIES: 13

POINTS TOTAL: 535

David Coulthard won a string of Scottish karting titles in the mid-1980s before progressing through the ranks of Formula Vauxhall, F3 and F3000. With no F1 drive on offer, 1994 looked set to be another F3000 campaign, but following Senna's death Coulthard was promoted from test driver to the Williams F1 team, partnering Damon Hill. He amassed 14 points from eight starts, the highlight a superb 2nd place in Estoril, before being replaced by the returning Nigel Mansell for the final three races. Even so, it was the Scot who was offered a seat for the 1995 campaign.

150 races with McLaren

Eight podiums earned him 3rd place in the 1995 title race. Coulthard joined McLaren in 1996, the beginning of a nine-year association that would encompass 150 races, a record for a driver with one team. Initially, the McLarens were a long way off the pace set by the team he had just left. He slipped to 7th in the 1996 rankings, but two wins in 1997, at Melbourne and Monza, helped him to equal 3rd in that season's title race.

McLaren had the car to win the championship in both 1998 and 1999, and did so courtesy of Mika Hakkinen. Coulthard won three races during this period and although he was a regular on the podium it was only good enough for 3rd and 4th respectively.

By 2001 he had emerged from Hakkinen's shadow, but Schumacher's time had come. By 2003 Kimi Räikkönen had taken over as McLaren's front runner, and at the end of the following year Coulthard left to sign for the Red Bull Racing Team. In 2006 he achieved the team's first podium finish at Monaco, where he came in 3rd. He ended the 2007 season in 10th place after amassing 14 points.

Podium finish in swansong year

Coulthard announced that he would retire at the end of the 2008 season. He got into the points only twice in his swansong year, but there was a final flourish at the Canadian GP, where he made it onto the podium for the 62nd time.

Juan Manuel Fangio

B. 24 June 1911, Balcarce, Argentina

D. 17 July 1995

Grand Prix starts: 51

Grand Prix victories: 24

Points total: 277.14

World champion 1951, 1954, 1955, 1956, 1957

Juan Manuel Fangio was 37 when, with financial backing from the Perón government, he left South America to try his hand on the racetracks of Europe in 1949. Beyond his native shores Fangio was an unknown quantity, but six wins in ten starts changed all that. Alfa Romeo was first out of the blocks when it came to gaining his signature for the inaugural world championship. His team-mates were Farina and Fagioli, and 'The Three Fs' dominated the series. Fangio won all three races in which his car went the distance. Unfortunately, the championship decider – Monza – was one in which he failed to reach the finish line. Farina won, overturning the four-point lead Fangio held going into the race. Fangio added three more wins to his tally in 1951, and also went into the final round, the Spanish GP, holding the advantage. This time he won comfortably, to claim the first of his five world titles.

Two championships with Mercedes

A broken neck at Monza sidelined Fangio for 1952, and he made his comeback the following year with Maserati. He won the Italian GP but it was Ascari and Ferrari's year.

Fangio had two more successes in a Maserati at the beginning of the 1954 season, a fine effort as he was only marking

time while his new team, Mercedes, was putting the finishing touches to its car. The stunning W196 was ready in time for Reims, where Fangio gave it a maiden victory. Three more wins followed in a car that appeared in both streamlined form – sporting a full-width body kit – and with open-wheel styling. With Fangio at the wheel the results were invariably the same.

1955 brought four more victories in a season truncated by the tragic events at Le Mans. One of the races in which he failed to cross the line first was at Aintree. He finished 0.2 seconds behind Moss, prompting speculation that he had gifted his team-mate a home victory.

Collins helps Fangio lift crown

Fangio's fourth world title, with Ferrari in 1956, is best remembered for the magnanimity of team-mate Peter Collins. Twice Fangio took over Collins' car to score points. The second occassion came in the decider at Monza, when Collins himself had a chance of lifting the title. A shared 2nd behind Moss that day gave him the championship by three points.

It was back to Maserati for 1957, and four wins in the first five European rounds set up his fifth world title. His victory at the Nurburgring, in which he carved 15 seconds off the lap record, is regarded as one of the greatest performances ever. He bowed out midway through the 1958 campaign, with a victories-to-starts ratio of almost 50 per cent.

Giuseppe Farina

B. 30 OCTOBER 1906, TURIN, ITALY
D. 30 JUNE 1966
GRAND PRIX STARTS: 33
GRAND PRIX VICTORIES: 5
POINTS TOTAL: 127.33
WORLD CHAMPION 1950

A member of the famous coachbuilding family, Giuseppe Farina was a protégé of Tazio Nuvolari in the 1930s. When Nuvolari left Alfa Romeo to join Auto Union in 1937, Farina became the team's no. 1, winning a hat-trick of Italian championships prior to the outbreak of WWII. After the war he drove Maseratis and Ferraris, but returned to Alfa on the eve of the new drivers' championship. He won the very first race, held at Silverstone on 13 May 1950, but trailed team-mate Fangio by four points going into the final round. The Argentine retired, and Farina crossed the line first to snatch the title by three points.

Move to Ferrari

The tables were turned the following year, Farina winning just once and slipping to 4th in the title race, twelve points behind Fangio. Alfa's withdrawal from racing allowed Farina to move to Ferrari for 1952. He was a regular runner-up to team-mate Ascari, and unsurprisingly finished 2nd in the championship. It was much the same story the following season, though his famous straight-arm driving style did produce a splendid win at the Nurburgring, Farina finishing over a minute ahead of Fangio's Maserati.

Terrible burns

Ascari's departure in 1954 left Farina as Ferrari's no. 1 but his season was blighted by injury. Having finished 2nd to Fangio in Argentina, he sustained a broken arm in the Mille Miglia. Farina drove at Spa with his arm in plaster, then suffered terrible burns during a sports-car race at Monza. He returned in 1955, driving through the pain barrier to finish 5th in that year's championship. He retired from F1 at the end of the year but retained an active interest in the sport. He was killed in a road accident while on his way to watch the 1966 French GP.

Emerson Fittipaldi

B. 12 DECEMBER 1946, SÃO PAULO, BRAZIL

GRAND PRIX STARTS: 144

GRAND PRIX VICTORIES: 14

POINTS TOTAL: 281

WORLD CHAMPION 1972, 1974

At 25 years and 298 days, Emerson Fittipaldi became the youngest ever world champion in 1972. Michael Schumacher was 16 days older when he won his first crown in 1994.

Within two years of arriving in Britain, Fittipaldi had impressed enough to earn a F1 berth with Lotus. He finished 4th behind team-mate Jochen Rindt at Hockenheim in 1970, despite running an outdated model. Following Rindt's death, Fittipaldi drove the superior Lotus 72 to victory at the US GP. His maiden win came in only his fourth start.

Fittipaldi lifts crown with JPS

The Brazilian enhanced his reputation in 1971, despite managing just 16 points. A year later Lotus fielded an upgraded version of the Lotus 72 – the John Player Special – and Fittipaldi swept to the championship with five victories. The last of those, at Monza, gave him the crown with two races to spare. Former champion Jackie Stewart won both of those races for Tyrell to finish runner-up, and the following year their positions were reversed. Fittipaldi won three races but had to settle for runner-up to the Scot.

Wins showdown with Regazzoni

Fittipaldi moved to McLaren for 1974, and Stewart's retirement meant that his chief rival of the past two seasons was off the scene. Three wins took Fittipaldi into a final-race showdown at Watkins Glen with Ferrari's Clay Regazzoni. The two were locked together in the points table, with Tyrell's Scheckter also in contention. Fourth place gave Fittipaldi his second championship, both of his rivals failing to score.

After finishing runner-up again in 1975, this time to Niki Lauda, Fittipaldi joined his brother's Copersucar team. There were a couple of podiums over the next five years but the cars were off the pace compared with the top F1 teams. He came out of retirement to take the Indy Car title in 1989, winning the Indy 500 that year and in 1993.

Timo Glock

B. 10 MARCH 1982, LINDENFEIS, GERMANY

GRAND PRIX STARTS: 22*

GRAND PRIX VICTORIES: 0*

POINTS TOTAL: 27*

*TO END OF 2008 SEASON

Over the years the German F3 championship has been a fertile breeding ground for future F1 drivers, most notably one Michael Schumacher, who took the title in 1990. Timo Glock competed in that series in 2002, following four successful years in karting. He took 3rd place and the Rookie of the Year award, and confirmed his promise by finishing 5th in the European F3 championship in 2003.

An exclusive club

Glock signed as test driver for Jordan for the new season, and stepped into the hot seat at the Canadian GP, taking over from a struggling Giorgio Pantano. He joined an exclusive club by scoring on his debut, though his 7th place did come at the expense of Williams and Toyota, whose cars were disqualified for brake irregularities. That might have been a stroke of good fortune, but Glock still crossed the line ahead of his more experienced team-mate Nick Heidfeld, and before the year was out he had taken Pantano's berth.

F2 champion

Jordan was in a state of flux, about to be sold to the Midland Group, and 2005 saw Glock competing in the Champ Car series. Second was his best finish – 8th overall – but he again took the top rookie honour. It was back to Europe and GP2 for the next two seasons, Glock lifting the title in 2007.

A replacement for Ralf Schumacher

He was also back on the F1 radar as test driver for BMW Sauber, but Toyota stole a march on several interested parties by signing him to replace Ralf Schumacher, who was leaving F1 for touring cars. The highlight of 2008 came at the Hungaroring, where he qualified 5th and finished 2nd to Kovaleinen's McLaren. His season's haul was 25 points, only six behind his vastly experienced team-mate Jarno Trulli, and he finished just behind the Italian in the final standings.

José Froilán González

B. 5 OCTOBER 1922, ARECIFES, ARGENTINA

GRAND PRIX STARTS: 26

GRAND PRIX VICTORIES: 2

POINTS TOTAL: 77.64

The man known as the 'Pampas Bull' followed in Fangio's footsteps, performing well enough in his native Argentina to earn the backing that allowed him to try his hand in Europe just as the inaugural world championship was gearing up. He drew a blank in the Maserati run by Scuderia Achille Varzi in 1950, but a move to Ferrari the following year brought a dramatic improvement, González running his illustrious compatriot close for that year's world title. His victory at Silverstone on 14 July 1951 ended a nine-race unbeaten run for Alfa Romeo in the championship. It was also Ferrari's maiden success. González brought the Ferrari 375 home in a podium position five races running, to finish the season 3rd overall.

Runner-up to Fangio

He spent the next two seasons at Maserati, the second of those with Fangio as his team-mate, but minor placings and a top-ten spot in the championship were all he could manage. A return to Ferrari in 1954 yielded his best return – runner-up to Fangio, albeit a long way off the pace set by his compatriot. González won the British GP again on his way to heading a powerful Maranello challenge, the line-up oncluding Hawthorn, Trintignant and the inaugural champion Farina. Although he won a number of non-championship F1 races and Le Mans, González retained a special affection for Silverstone, the scene of his only two wins in the blue riband series.

No Silverstone hat-trick

González mainly restricted his appearances to the Argentinian GP. In 1956 there was a shared 2nd place in Buenos Aires, behind his usual nemesis Fangio. That season he also found the lure of Silverstone too great but there was to be no glorious hat-trick: a broken driveshaft meant that he didn't even complete one lap. He then retired to concentrate on his garage business.

Mika Hakkinen

B. 28 SEPTEMBER 1968, HELSINKI, FINLAND

GRAND PRIX STARTS: 165

GRAND PRIX VICTORIES: 20

POINTS TOTAL: 420

WORLD CHAMPION 1998, 1999

Mika Hakkinen took over from Keke Rosberg as Finland's F1 star. He won the British F3 title in 1990, graduating to F1 with Lotus the following season. The Judd-engined car was well off the pace, though he did bring it home 5th at Imola to register his first points. He scored in six races in '92, to finish a highly creditable 8th in the championship. Fourth place at Magny-Cours took the eye, and it was clear that with a better car Hakkinen had the ability to challenge the best. He joined McLaren, though initially had to kick his heels behind Senna and Michael Andretti. It was only after the latter was fired that Hakkinen got his chance. In just his second start, Suzuka, he finished 3rd behind Senna and Prost.

Life-threatening injuries

1994 yielded six podiums, earning Hakkinen 4th place in the championship. He sustained life-threatening head injuries at the 1995 Australian GP, but recovered to finish 5th in the next two seasons. He got his long-awaited victory at Jerez, the final round of the 1997 championship, though he was helped by Villeneuve, who reined in his Williams knowing that 3rd was enough for him to win the title.

Wins showdown with Ferrari

Having waited so long for a victory, they then came thick and fast. Hakkinen topped the podium eight times in 1998 to claim the crown, then won five times in 1999 in defence of the title. In both years it went to the final race: he held off Schumacher's challenge in 1998, then when injury forced the German out of the running in 1999, Hakkinen had the edge on his Ferrari team-mate Eddie Irvine.

There were four wins in 2000, one of them after a dazzling 200-mph battle with Schumacher at Spa, but this time he finished runner-up to the German. His swansong F1 season yielded two more victories, in Britain and the US, a year in which he slipped to 5th in the title race.

Lewis Hamilton

B. 7 JANUARY 1985, STEVENAGE, ENGLAND

GRAND PRIX STARTS: 35*

GRAND PRIX VICTORIES: 9*

POINTS TOTAL: 207*

WORLD CHAMPION 2008

*TO END OF 2008 SEASON

After winning the British Cadet championship in 1995, 10-year-old Lewis Hamilton knew that he wanted to drive in F1 for McLaren, following in the footsteps of his hero, Ayrton Senna. In fact, just three years went by before Dennis's team took the karting prodigy under its wing.

The honours came thick and fast: European Champion and World Cup Champion in Formula A in 2000; Formula Renault UK Champion in 2003 and F3 Euroseries Champion in 2005. For 2006 it was on to GP2 with the ART team, where he took the title after battling with Nelson Piquet Junior.

F1 debut

McLaren confirmed his F1 seat for 2007, alongside double world champion Fernando Alonso. Elated but not overawed, Hamilton made a blistering start to his rookie year at the top table, with nine straight podium finishes, including back-to-back wins in Canada and the USA. He headed the championship race from Round Three until the final twist at Interlagos, where Kimi Räikkönen's victory was enough to snatch the crown by a single point. Hamilton was philosophical about the defeat, which he took with great humility. At 22 he had become the youngest driver to lead the championship, breaking Bruce McLaren's record, and knew his talent and extraordinary focus would give him many more tilts at the title.

Youngest ever champion

Hamilton had to wait just one year to put the disappointment of 2007 behind him. It was another championship that went to the wire, a last-gasp overtaking manoeuvre at Interlagos securing him 5th place, enough to snatch the title from Ferrari's Felipe Massa by one point. At 23 years 301 days he became the youngest ever Formula One champion, taking the record from Fernando Alonso, who was 122 days older when he was crowned in 2005.

Mike Hawthorn

B. 10 APRIL 1929, MEXBOROUGH, ENGLAND

D. 22 JANUARY 1959

GRAND PRIX STARTS: 45

GRAND PRIX VICTORIES: 3

POINTS TOTAL: 127.64

WORLD CHAMPION 1958

The blond, flamboyant Mike Hawthorn cut a dashing figure on the racing scene in the 1950s. Although he invariably competed in a cap and bow-tie, his dapper appearance belied his fierce competitiveness and the fact that he served a long apprenticeship before winning the world crown.

By 1952, when he made his GP debut at Spa, Hawthorn was already seen as a rising star. He enhanced his reputation by finishing 3rd at Silverstone on the way to taking joint 4th place in the championship. He drove for a team run by father Leslie, but for 1953 he was snapped up by Ferrari. His first GP victory came at Reims

that year, Hawthorn outbraking Fangio at the final corner in a breathtaking manoeuvre. He again finished 4th, having shown great consistency as well as courage and skill.

Hawthorn involved in Le Mans tragedy

The 1954 campaign was blighted by an accident at the non-championship Syracuse GP, but Hawthorn recovered to win the Spanish GP and finish 3rd overall. He briefly joined Vanwall in 1955 a decision prompted by his father's death and the need to oversee the family business – before rejoining Ferrari. The championship races proved fruitless, but he did win at Le Mans in a Jaguar. Victory was tainted by an accident which resulted in 82 deaths, Hawthorn coming in for criticism for the manoeuvre that precipitated the tragic incident.

Pips Moss for title

After a forgettable 1956 season Hawthorn returned to form, reunited once again with Ferrari. 1958 was the crowning glory. He won only once, the French GP, but scored consistently to pip Moss for the title by a single point.

Hawthorn announced his retirement almost immediately. He was deeply affected by the death of team-mate Peter Collins and was also suffering from a debilitating kidney condition. He was killed in a road accident on 22 January 1959, just three months after becoming Britain's first world champion.

Nick Heidfeld

B. 10 May 1977, Mönchengladbach, Germany

Grand Prix starts: 153*

Grand Prix victories: 4*

Points total: 200*

* to end of 2008 season

Nick Heidfeld went into the 2009 season, his 10th in F1, with more than 150 races and 11 podium finishes under his belt but still seeking that elusive first victory. He won the German Formula Ford title aged 17 in 1994, following six years on the karting circuit. He lifted the German F3 title in 1997, and no doubt hoped to emulate the achievements of Michael Schumacher, who had scooped the same honour seven years before. By the following year he was in McLaren's sights as part of their driver development programme, but after a spell as test driver he was passed over by Ron Dennis's team. In 1999 he won the International Formula 3000 title, avenging the narrow defeat he suffered at the hands of Juan Pablo Montoya in the same championship a year earlier.

Success for Sauber

A struggling Prost team handed him his first F1 start in 2000, and neither he nor veteran Jean Alesi could muster a single point. Heidfeld moved on to Sauber in 2001, partnering young rookie Kimi Räikkönen. He got his first taste of a top-three finish that year, finishing behind Coulthard and Michael Schumacher at Interlagos to give Sauber its first podium for three years. He outscored Räikkönen, but it was the latter who got the call from McLaren at the year end. Fourth place in Spain and an aggregate seven points was the best Heidfeld could manage in 2002, though it was a better return than that of new partner Felipe Massa. After one more season with Sauber, Heidfeld joined a Jordan team in decline and struggled all year with an uncompetitive car.

A move to Williams

He saw his 2005 move to Williams as the chance he had been waiting for, and two early-season 2nd places were promising indicators. Injury forced him to miss the last five races, though he still managed 28 points and 11th place in the championship. 2006 saw Heidfeld join the new BMW Sauber enterprise. He scored in 10 rounds, though mostly just edging into the points. The next two years were a different matter. Heidfeld had 13 top-six finishes to take 5th place in the 2007 championship, and fell just one point and one place short of that career-best return in 2008.

Damon Hill

B. 17 SEPTEMBER 1960, LONDON, ENGLAND
GRAND PRIX STARTS: 114
GRAND PRIX VICTORIES: 22
POINTS TOTAL: 360
WORLD CHAMPION 1996

When Damon Hill began racing competitively in the late 1970s, inevitably he was compared with his illustrious father. He overcame the intense media scrutiny and pressure of being the son of one of the sport's legends to carve his own place in motor racing's hall of fame.

Hill's first love was motorcycles, and his first forays into four-wheeled racing in the early 1980s were not a resounding success. Between 1986 and 1988 he competed in the British F3 championship, improving each year to finish 3rd in his final campaign.

Test driver for Williams

There followed three years in F3000, where again progress was steady rather than spectacular. Hill hadn't had the best cars at his disposal, however, and the fact that he had shown himself to be a genuine racer despite mediocre hardware helped secure a test-driving contract at Williams.

Brabham handed him his F1 debut in 1992, a disastrous season in which Hill struggled to qualify, let alone register a championship point. Testing with Williams went much better and for 1993 he was promoted to no. 2 behind Prost. After a series of podiums Hill scored a start-to-finish victory in Hungary and followed it up with two more wins for 3rd place in the title race.

Promoted to no. 1 after Senna's death

Senna replaced Prost the following year, but after the Brazilian's death at Imola Hill became Williams' no. 1. He rose to the challenge magnificently, fighting an attritional battle with Michael Schumacher. It ended in the final race, Adelaide, with the German's Benetton rebounding off a wall and taking Hill out of the race to clinch the championship by a point.

He was runner-up again in 1995, but the following season Hill took the world crown, scoring eight victories in the 16-race series. Even before the title was his Hill knew he and Williams were parting company. A season with Arrows followed by two years with Jordan produced just one victory, after which Hill announced his retirement.

Graham Hill

B. 15 FEBRUARY 1929, HAMPSTEAD LONDON
D. 29 NOVEMBER 1975
GRAND PRIX STARTS: 176
GRAND PRIX VICTORIES: 14
POINTS TOTAL: 289
WORLD CHAMPION 1962, 1968

The handsome, urbane Graham Hill was a raconteur and wit as well as an outstanding driver. His extrovert character was very different from that of his great rival, Jim Clark, yet the two shared a steely resolve. Clark arrived at Lotus in 1960, the year Hill departed for BRM, desperate for a car that would give him the platform to win the world title.

Hill accumulated just seven points in his first two seasons with BRM, but by 1962 the car had a new V8 unit and results improved dramatically. Hill's maiden victory came in the opening race, Zandvoort, and wins in Germany and Italy put him nine points clear of Clark going into the final race. Clark could have won the title with a victory and looked on course to do just that until his Lotus failed at the three-quarter distance. Hill won the race and took the crown.

Ferrari tactics rob Hill of title

Hill finished runner-up in the next three championship series. In 1963 and 1965 he finished well behind Clark, but 1964 was a different story. He went into the final race five points clear of Ferrari's John Surtees. Hill was well down the field, and had to hope that Surtees finished no better than 3rd. Surtees' team-mate Lorenzo Bandini let him through to take 2nd, and with it the six points he needed to secure the championship by a point.

Cosworth engine brings second crown

Hill had a disappointing 1966 championship, the year of the new 3-litre formula, although he did win the Indy 500. In 1967 he rejoined Lotus, and when the new Cosworth DFV engine arrived mid-season, the team looked set for an assault on the 1968 championship. Following team-mate Clark's death early in the season, Hill assumed the responsibility of team leader. He restored the morale of a shattered Lotus camp with three victories on the way to a second world title.

The blue riband treble

Hill slid down the rankings in 1969, although he did register his fifth Monaco victory. He sustained severe leg injuries in a crash at Watkins Glen and, although he recovered to drive a privateer Lotus in 1970, his best days were behind him. Two fruitless seasons with Brabham followed, although in 1972 he did win at Le Mans. He remains the only man to complete the blue riband treble: the world championship, the Indy 500 and Le Mans.

Hill retired in 1975 to concentrate on establishing his own team. Returning from testing at Paul Ricard on 29 November that year, he and five team members were killed when the plane he was piloting crashed in fog near Elstree.

Phil Hill

B. 20 APRIL 1927, MIAMI, USA

D. 28 AUGUST 2008

GRAND PRIX STARTS: 48

GRAND PRIX VICTORIES: 3

POINTS TOTAL: 98

WORLD CHAMPION 1961

Phil Hill was successful in sports cars, and also won Le Mans, before turning his attention to F1. He made his debut at the 1958 French GP, running a Maserati owned by Jo Bonnier, and finished 7th, one place ahead of the Swede. He had already caught the eye of Enzo Ferrari, however, and was soon signed to the Maranello stable, where he spent the next four years and made steady progress. Two 2nd places, in France and Italy, elevated him to 4th in the 1959 championship. He dropped one place the following season, chiefly because Ferrari persisted with the front-engined D246 when the rest of F1 had seen that rear-engined machines were the way forward. Given that handicap, Hill did well to win at Monza, although his cause was helped by the fact that the dominant British teams boycotted a race held on the famous banked track for safety reasons.

Hill and 'sharknose' dominate

Having lagged the field in 1960, Ferrari stole a march on its rivals with the introduction of the new 1.5-litre formula in 1961. The V6 'sharknose' was the car to beat, and by the penultimate race, Monza, the championship looked set to be a fight between Ferrari team-mates Hill and Wolfgang von Trips. The German clashed with Jim Clark's Lotus on the first lap and was killed, along with twelve spectators. The tragedy overshadowed the fact that Hill won the race and with it the title.

Joins Ferrari breakaway team

Ferrari fell behind the British marques in 1962, which proved to be a disppointment for Hill. He joined a Ferrari splinter group which left to set up ATS in 1963, but failed to notch a single point. A season with Cooper was scarcely better, yielding only a 6th place at Brands Hatch. Thereafter Hill concentrated on sports car racing, though ill-health forced him to retire in 1967.

46

Denny Hulme

B. 18 MARCH 1936, NELSON, NEW ZEALAND

D. 4 OCTOBER 1992

GRAND PRIX STARTS: 112

GRAND PRIX VICTORIES: 8

POINTS TOTAL: 248

WORLD CHAMPION 1967

Denny Hulme travelled to Britain in 1960 to compete in Formula Junior. A year later he went to work as a mechanic for Jack Brabham's fledgling Motor Racing Developments, the start of a long and successful association. Hulme drove works Brabhams in Formula Junior, the Tasman series and F2, before being promoted to the top team in 1965. He made his debut at Monaco, replacing Dan Gurney, who was competing at Indianapolis. He finished 8th that day, but two races later, Brabham made way for Hulme at Clermont-Ferrand, and the New Zealander repaid the boss with 4th place.

Beats team boss to title

In 1966 Gurney followed Brabham's lead in setting up his own outfit, leaving Hulme as official no. 2. The Brabham-Repco was ahead of the game in the new 3-litre era, and while Brabham won his third title, Hulme got on the podium four times to secure 4th place in the championship. A year later it was the Kiwi's turn. The Cosworth DFV was about to take F1 by storm, but Brabham had one more season of dominance. At Monaco he took the lead after Ferrari's Lorenzo Bandini crashed fatally, and went on to score his maiden victory. Hulme led a Brabham one-two at the Nurburgring, though only after former team-mate Dan Gurney's Eagle failed with three laps to go. Third place in the final race, the Mexican GP, was enough to give Hulme the title from Brabham.

Seven years at McLaren

Hulme chose the right moment to leave Brabham for McLaren, taking two more wins to finish 3rd in the 1968 championship. He remained with his compatriot's outfit for six more years, until his retirement from F1 in 1974. There were just four more wins in that period. 1972 was his best year, a 39-point haul putting 36-year-old Hulme 3rd behind Fittipaldi and Stewart. He died from a heart attack while competing in Australia's Bathurst touring-car race in 1992.

James Hunt

B. 29 AUGUST 1947, BELMONT, ENGLAND

D. 15 JUNE 1993

GRAND PRIX STARTS: 92

GRAND PRIX VICTORIES: 10

POINTS TOTAL: 179

WORLD CHAMPION 1976

The flamboyant, pugnacious James Hunt turned his back on a professional career to pursue his passion for motor racing. He resorted to supermarket shelf-stacking to finance his early forays into the sport, which began with a humble Mini. He moved on to Formula Ford and F3, where there were some notable victories but also many spills, leading the tabloids to apply the 'Hunt the Shunt' tag.

Hunt signed for the March F3 team in 1972, but before the year was out he had departed to join forces with Lord Hesketh's maverick outfit. It was on to F2 almost immediately, and, when he managed to keep clear of trouble, Hunt showed that he had the speed to handle the step up in class.

Victory over Lauda brings maiden success

In 1973 Hesketh launched an assault on F1. A Ford-engined March 731 was procured and Hunt was soon in the points. The highlight was the final race of the year, Watkins Glen, where he finished 2nd behind Ronnie Peterson. fourteen points in total gave Hunt a highly respectable 8th place in the championship. He matched that

performance the following season, this time in the team's own car, the Ford-powered Hesketh 308. Improvements to the car yielded even greater dividends in 1975. Hunt amassed 33 points to finish 4th, splitting the Ferraris, McLarens and Brabhams. That season also saw him beat eventual champion Niki Lauda into second place at Zandvoort to score his maiden victory.

Hunt joins McLaren

Financial troubles led Hesketh to withdraw at the end of the year, and Hunt replaced Emerson Fittipaldi at McLaren. 1976 was a thrilling series, Hunt and Ferrari's Lauda engaged in a battle which went to the wire. His first win for McLaren came at Spain, although there was an anxious wait before a protest involving the M23's dimensions was overruled. A further investigation followed Hunt's victory in a restarted race at Silverstone. This time the rules had been infringed and his points were expunged. Lauda's enforced absence following his horrific accident at the Nurburgring brought Hunt back into contention, and he went into the final race, the Japanese GP, three points behind the Austrian. Appalling conditions prompted Lauda to withdraw, and Hunt went on a furious charge to secure the 3rd place he needed to clinch the title.

Swaps racetrack for commentary box

There were three more victories in 1977, but McLaren was in decline. 1978 was even worse and Hunt appeared to lose motivation and enthusiasm. A brief spell at Wolf in 1979 brought no improvement and he quit mid-season.

Hunt went on to become one of the voices of F1 in the TV commentatry box, a job he discharged with aplomb until his death from a heart attack on 15 June 1993.

Jacky Ickx

B. 1 JANUARY 1945, BRUSSELS, BELGIUM

GRAND PRIX STARTS: 116

GRAND PRIX VICTORIES: 8

POINTS TOTAL: 181

Jacky Ickx emerged as one of motor racing's brightest young talents in the 1960s. He went from trials riding, hill climbs to saloon cars in rapid succession, starring in each and winning his home championship in the saloon class in 1965. Ken Tyrell signed him, promoting him from F3 to F2, then giving him his world championship debut in the 1966 German GP, albeit in an F2 Matra-Ford.

In 1967 he divided his time, winning the European F2 title while making the occasional F1 appearance. He qualified his F2 car 3rd at the Nurburgring, but in accordance with the rules had to start from the back of the grid with the other F2 entries. He carved his way through to 4th before his suspension gave out. Two races later he turned out for Cooper at Monza, finishing 6th to gain his first championship point.

Runner-up to Stewart

A move to Ferrari followed, and he comfortably outpaced team-mate Chris Amon to finish 4th in the title race. He gave Maranello their only win of the season, at Rouen in the wet. Ickx was now a hot property, and when Rindt left Brabham for Lotus, the Belgian was drafted in as replacement. Brabham had finally abandoned the Repco unit and joined the DFV bandwagon, and Ickx had a fine year, winning in Germany and Canada to finish runner-up to Stewart, and also adding a Le Mans victory to his cv.

Sixth Le Mans victory

It was back to Ferrari for the next four years. There were five more wins over the first three seasons, but after finishing runner-up in 1970, the car became increasingly uncompetitive. He quit midway through the 1973 series and the following year joined Lotus. His two seasons there yielded an aggregate 15 points. From 1976 to 1979 there were sporadic outings for Williams, Ensign and Ligier but to little avail. Thereafter he concentrated on sports cars, winning Le Mans for a sixth time in 1982.

Eddie Irvine

B. 10 NOVEMBER 1965, NEWTOWNARDS, NORTHERN IRELAND

GRAND PRIX STARTS: 146

GRAND PRIX VICTORIES: 4

POINTS TOTAL: 191

Eddie Irvine made his GP debut in 1993 for Jordan, the team for which he had earlier performed well in F3000. That baptism, at Suzuka, was remarkable enough for producing the Ulsterman's first championship point; it was even more noteworthy for the spat with race winner Ayrton Senna, who took exception to an overtaking manoeuvre from a driver he had already lapped. The two came to blows afterwards, an indication that the self-assured Irvine stood in awe or fear of no one.

Ban follows pile-up

More controversy followed the 1994 curtain-raiser, Interlagos, where Irvine received a one-race ban for his part in a pile-up. His devil-may-care attitude at the subsequent appeal no doubt contributed to the ban being increased threefold. Fourth place in the European GP at Jerez was the highlight of some fine late-season displays.

Irvine got on to the podium for the first time at the 1995 Canadian GP, but in the championship Jordan was a long way off the pace. In 1996 he got the opportunity to prove himself at a premier team when he signed for Ferrari. Michael Schumacher also moved to Maranello, however, and Irvine inevitably had to play second fiddle.

Team backing after Schumacher injury

It was more of the same in 1997, Irvine picking up useful points, including a fine 2nd in Argentina, but always conscious of the supporting role that was expected of him.

Increasing in confidence, Irvine notched 47 points to finish 4th in the 1998 title race. The following year, with Schumacher sidelined through injury, Irvine finally got full team backing. Three victories took him into the final round two points adrift of Mika Hakkinen. He was unable to overhaul the Finn but at least he had prevented a McLaren clean sweep.

Irvine left Ferrari in 2000 to spearhead Jaguar's assault on F1. Three seasons yielded only the occasional noteworthy result, and after scoring just eight points in 2002 his contract was not renewed.

Alan Jones

B. 2 NOVEMBER 1946, MELBOURNE, AUSTRALIA

GRAND PRIX STARTS: 116

GRAND PRIX VICTORIES: 12

POINTS TOTAL: 206

WORLD CHAMPION 1980

Alan Jones's father was a racer who always regretted never travelling to Europe to compete on the biggest stages. The tough, forthright Jones Jr wasn't about to end his career with the same regrets. After five years in the junior ranks, during which time he eked out a meagre existence, Jones got his F1 break, in a privately entered Hesketh. A few races later, injury to Rolf Stommelen created an opening at Graham Hill's Embassy Racing. He gave the fledgling team its best finish with a fifth place in Germany, but the deaths of Hill and a number of his team in a plane crash at the end of the year left Jones looking for a new challenge.

Joins Shadow after Pryce's death

He joined John Surtees, notching seven points in his one season there before walking away. He was back in action by the fourth race of the 1977 series, Long Beach, recruited by Shadow to replace Tom Pryce, who had been killed at Kyalami. After a couple of respectable points finishes, Jones scored a stunning success in Austria, both his and the team's first time atop the podium. He beat Lauda, who would go on to win the championship with Ferrari, leaving pundits wondering what the Australian might do with better equipment.

Jones and FW07 sweep to title

There was talk of him joining Maranello but in the end he linked up with Frank Williams and Patrick Head. When the FW07 was unveiled towards the end of the 1979 season, Jones reeled off four wins in five starts to finish 3rd in the championship. Five more wins helped him stave off the challenge of Brabham's Piquet in 1980, the year in which he took the crown and Williams their first Constructors' title.

Jones scored two more wins on his way to 3rd in the 1981 championship, then announced his retirement. He made two ill-judged comebacks which failed to do justice to his talent.

Heikki Kovaleinen

B. 19 OCTOBER 1981, SUOMUSSAIMI, FINLAND

GRAND PRIX STARTS: 35*

GRAND PRIX VICTORIES: 1*

POINTS TOTAL: 83*

*TO END OF 2008 SEASON

Heikki Kovaleinen spent a long apprenticeship on the karting scene in his homeland, culminating in his becoming Nordic champion in 2000. He took the Elf Masters title the same year, his last before making the step up to car racing in the British Formula Renault series. He finished 4th in the 2001 championship, not quite as impressive as compatriot Kimi Räikkönen, who won the event the preceding year, but two wins did help bring him the Rookie of the Year award.

Rising star in F3

In 2002 Kovaleinen competed in the British F3 championship, taking 3rd place to confirm his reputation as one of the sport's rising stars. He played second fiddle to experienced team-mate Franck Montagny in the 2003 World Series by Nissan championship, but lifted the title the following year, driving for Pons Racing. 2004 also saw him win the individual title at the Race of Champions, beating David Coulthard and Michael Schumacher en route to victory in Paris. He was edged into second place by Nico Rosberg in a thrilling inaugural GP2 championship in 2005.

30 points in debut season

The following year he became Renault's main test driver, and when Fernando Alonso departed to McLaren at the end of a second title-winning campaign, Kovaleinen was promoted to the vacant race seat in 2007. He scored 30 points in his debut season in the elite division, the highlight coming at Fuji Speedway, where he fended off Räikkönen's attentions to take second behind Lewis Hamilton in a race run in appalling conditions. It was the Finn's first podium and Renault's best result of the year. Kovaleinen outpointed team-mate Giancarlo Fisichella.

Partnering Lewis Hamilton

When Renault welcomed Alonso back for the 2008 campaign, Kovaleinen was on the move, taking Alonso's McLaren berth. He was the junior partner as Lewis Hamilton mounted a successful title charge, but he did notch three more podium finishes, including a maiden victory at the Hungarian GP.

Robert Kubica

B. 7 DECEMBER 1984, KRAKOW, POLAND

GRAND PRIX STARTS: 40*

GRAND PRIX VICTORIES: 0*

POINTS TOTAL: 120*

*TO END OF 2008 SEASON

When Jacques Villeneuve announced he was quitting BMW Sauber midway through the 2006 season, he seemed to have predicted the way the wind was blowing. The former world champion's contract was up at the end of the year, and it became clear that the team was looking to promote 21-year-old test driver Robert Kubica. Kubica may have got the drive at the Hungarian GP only because Villeneuve hadn't fully recovered from a spill at Hockenheim, but it was obvious that the Pole represented the team's long-term future. Kubica finished 7th in Hungary, only to be disqualified when it was found his car was underweight. That took the edge off an impressive debut, though it was no surprise when he was installed as Villeneuve's long-term replacement.

Young talent

Kubica showed a prodigious talent behind the wheel from a young age, lifting six domestic karting titles before decamping to Italy, where competition was stiffer. He took that country's championship in 1998, the first non-Italian to receive those particular laurels. He picked up more karting honours over the next two years before switching to Formula Renault 2000. He went on to compete in the European F3 championship, but his biggest success came in 2005, when he took the World Series by Renault title. That earned him a test for Renault's F1 team, but it was BMW Sauber who enlisted his services for 2006, his breakthrough year.

Maiden victory in Canada

Kubica took 3rd place at Monza in 2006, stepping onto the podium in only his third race. He was regularly in the points in 2007 and finished 6th in the championship, despite a spectacular spill in Montreal which put him out of that race and the next. In 2008 he kept pace with the title contenders from McLaren and Ferrari, and when he scored his maiden victory in Canada, Kubica led the championship. He remained in contention for the crown until the penultimate round and finished the year level on points with Räikkönen, who edged him for 3rd place by dint of race wins.

Niki Lauda

B. 22 FEBRUARY 1949, VIENNA, AUSTRIA

GRAND PRIX STARTS: 171

GRAND PRIX VICTORIES: 25

POINTS TOTAL: 420.5

WORLD CHAMPION 1975, 1977, 1984

Niki Lauda's fireball accident at the Nurburgring in 1976 – and his return to the cockpit to finish 4th at Monza just six weeks later – is one of sport's most remarkable comebacks. Later, he chalked up another extraordinary achievement, becoming the only man to come out of retirement to reclaim the world crown.

Potential realized at Maranello

Lauda's first F1 outings were with March and in 1973 he moved to BRM for a season. Four glorious years at Ferrari followed. The Austrian had shown flashes of talent, but was still very much seen as raw potential. Team-mate Regazzoni outpointed him in the first season, 1974, the duo finishing 2nd and 4th respectively in the championship. But Lauda had won twice, the Swiss just once, and their positions were determined by the fact that Lauda suffered a number of retirements.

That all changed in 1975, Lauda winning five times to clinch the world crown with a race to spare. 1976 was all about the battle with Hunt and McLaren, and that crash at the Nurburgring. Lauda received last rites, yet was back to join battle at Monza, bearing terrible scars. Lauda led Hunt going into the final round, Suzuka, but walked away from a race that was run in appalling conditions. Hunt got the points he needed and Lauda finished runner-up.

Quits Ferrari after second title

He roared back in 1977, winning three more GPs en route to a second title with Ferrari and silencing the Italian fans who had criticized him for not racing in Japan. He then left to join Brabham. His first season produced a respectable 44 points and 4th place, Lauda winning in the famous 'fan car's' only outing, But 1979 was an unmitigated disaster, and the Austrian announced his retirement.

Two years later he was back, with McLaren. He topped the podium in just his third race, finishing 5th overall in the 1983 championship. The McLaren MP4 was disappointing in 1983, but a year later the new car blew away the opposition. Lauda's greatest challenge came from his new young team-mate Alain Prost. The Frenchman won the decider, Estoril, but Lauda's 2nd place gave him the title by half a point, the closest championship finish ever. He won his 25th and final GP at Zandvoort in 1985, retiring at the end of that season.

Nigel Mansell

B. 8 AUGUST 1953, UPTON-ON-SEVERN, ENGLAND	
GRAND PRIX STARTS: 187	
GRAND PRIX VICTORIES: 31	
POINTS TOTAL: 482	
WORLD CHAMPION 1992	

Nigel Mansell had the benefit of being behind the wheel of the all-conquering Williams FW14B during his glorious championship-winning season of 1992. Even so, it was a year of outstanding achievement, Mansell taking pole in all but two of the races and winning nine of them to become the first man to rack up over a century of points. Nearest rival Riccardo Patrese, his Williams team-mate, finished a staggering 52 points behind.

F1 debut for Lotus

For Mansell 1992 was the crowning glory of more than two decades in competitive motor sport. He made his F1 debut for Lotus in 1980, at the Austrian GP. There he raced through the pain of petrol burns until retiring, an indication of the indomitable spirit for which he would become renowned.

Mansell spent four more seasons at Lotus, during which time his great mentor, Colin Chapman, died. His last year with the team, 1984, gave him his best return thus far, a modest 13 points. A move to Williams the following season transformed his career. Two victories, at the European and South African GPs, helped him to a 31-point haul and 6th place in the championship.

Blown tyre hands title to Prost

It was runner-up for the next two seasons. In 1986 he went into the final race six points clear of Prost, but a blown tyre allowed the Frenchman to pip him for the crown. Having scored five wins that year, he went one better in 1987 but lost out to team-mate Nelson Piquet. A crash during qualifying for Suzuka put paid to his chances.

The loss of the Honda engine blighted the 1988 campaign, and although there were three wins during a two-year stint at Ferrari, Mansell was out of contention for the title. He considered retirement but was lured back to Williams in 1991, when he finished runner-up for the third time. The Williams, now powered by a Renault unit, was once again competitive, but a tally of five wins wasn't quite enough to outdo Senna.

Indy-car champion

After his glory year Mansell left to try his hand in Indy-cars, winning the 1993 championship. In 1994 he made a dramatic return to F1 and Williams following Senna's death, recording his 31st and final win at Adelaide. With Hill and Coulthard occupying the berths at Williams for 1995, Mansell began the season with McLaren but quit after just two races. This time retirement was permanent.

Mansell stands 4th in the all-time list for GP victories, while only Schumacher, Prost, Senna and Piquet have scored more championship points.

Felipe Massa

B. 25 April 1981, São Paulo, Brazil

Grand Prix starts: 105*

Grand Prix victories: 11*

Points total: 298*

*to end of 2008 season

For a few brief moments at Interlagos on 2 November 2008 the Ferrari camp thought Felipe Massa had secured the world crown but Lewis Hamilton spoiled the party with his last-gasp manoeuvre that saw him pass Timo Glock to snatch 5th place, and with it the title by a single point. Massa hid his disappointment and congratulated the new champion in a display of magnanimity that was a fitting template for all sportsmen. 'I know how to lose and I know how to win,' said the Brazilian ace. He certainly showed the winning mentality in 2008, outgunning Hamilton 6–5 in terms of top-of-the-podium finishes, and he had the consolation of helping Ferrari to yet another Constructors' title.

An invitation from Sauber

São Paulo-born Massa had seven years in karting before stepping up to Formula Chevrolet at the age of 17. By 2002 he had earned an invitation from Sauber to join the F1 ranks, replacing the departing Räikkönen. That proved a steep learning curve. He spent the following year as a Ferrari test driver, and he was older and wiser when he returned to Sauber in 2004, helped by the fact that the team was using Ferrari power. He garnered 12 points, with a best-place finish of 4th in an accident-ridden race at Spa. There was a similar return in 2005, the year in which Peter Sauber sold out to BMW, after which Massa moved to Ferrari to take over Barrichello's long-held number two berth to Michael Schumacher.

Driving for Ferrari

Schumacher and Alonso fought a ding-dong battle in 2006, but Massa was the best of the rest, albeit 41 points adrift of his team-mate. That campaign was notable for his first two victories, scored in Istanbul and in his home race. It was Schumacher's swansong year, and Massa found himself partnering Räikkönen in 2007. There were three more victories, though he eventually finished 4th in a Ferrari-McLaren duel that went to the wire. Räikkönen snatched the championship from rivals Hamilton and Alonso in the final race in Brazil.

A genuine contender

A year later it was the Finn who was out of contention and pushing for a Massa victory. The cards didn't fall right for Felipe in 2008, but in taking the runner-up spot he had shown that he was no supporting act but a genuine contender.

Bruce McLaren

B. 30 AUGUST 1937, AUCKLAND, NEW ZEALAND	
D. 2 JUNE 1970	
GRAND PRIX STARTS: 101	
GRAND PRIX VICTORIES: 4	
POINTS TOTAL: 196.5	

It took Jack Brabham four years to win his first Grand Prix after coming to Europe. Black Jack's fellow antipodean and protégé Bruce McLaren topped the rostrum within a year of his arrival. McLaren won a scholarship in New Zealand to enable him to contest the European Formula Two series in 1958, in a works Cooper. He made his F1 debut at the Nurburgring that year, winning the F2 class and finishing 5th overall.

A full campaign followed, Mclaren winning at Sebring to become the youngest ever GP winner, a record which still stands. He was 22 years 104 days old. That victory helped him to 6th place in the championship, and the following season he pushed Brabham hard, eventually finishing runner-up to his Cooper team-mate.

Cooper's No.1 following Brabham's exit
McLaren was Cooper's top scorer for the next five seasons, though for most of that time the cars were not among the front-runners. His best year was 1962, his first campaign as team leader following Brabham's departure to set up on his own. He won in Monaco and ended the year 3rd behind Hill and Clark.

In 1966 he followed Brabham's lead by fielding his own Robin Herd-designed car. It was the beginning of the 3-litre formula and the team struggled to find a decent engine for the M2B. Ironically, while McLaren tried several units, Brabham romped to his third championship with the superb Repco.

First win for a McLaren car
By 1968, when he lured reigning champion Denny Hulme from Brabham, the car had Cosworth DFV power. McLaren's fourth GP win, at Spa, was the first for the marque. It helped him to finish 5th in the championship. There were no victories in 1969, but consistent scoring put him 3rd in the table, while he also completed a hat-trick of CanAm titles. Having contested three rounds of the 1970 series – finishing second at Jarama – McLaren was killed while testing one of his CanAm cars at Goodwood.

Guy Moll

B. 1908, ALGERIA

D. 15 AUGUST 1934

Guy Moll's star shone extraordinarily brightly, albeit for just two years, one as a works driver. His brief period at the pinnacle of motor racing inevitably brought caveats that true greats sustain their form over an extended period. However, Enzo Ferrari certainly had no doubts as to Moll's calibre, putting him in the same class as Nuvolari.

Moll, born to a Spanish mother and French father, first took the eye when he drove his Bugatti to 3rd place behind Sommer and Nuvolari at the 1932 Marseille GP. The result was the more remarkable for the fact that he had only completed his studies that year. An absolute novice, he had turned to motor racing as an adventurous diversion and found he had an extraordinary aptitude behind the wheel.

Seven top-three finishes

The fillip of Marseille persuaded Moll to invest in a 2.3-litre Alfa Romeo Monza for the 1933 season. The car wasn't ready in time for the Pau GP, and Moll joined battle against appalling wintry conditions and the cream of European talent in an old T51 Bugatti. Only the veteran Marcel Lehoux, his mentor, got the better of him that day. He was 3rd at the Nice GP, by which time the new Alfa had arrived, and at the end of his first year of international racing he had seven top-three finishes to his name, although he was still looking for his first win.

Joins Ferrari

His performances attracted the attention of Enzo Ferrari, who drafted Moll into his 1934 team, at the time running Alfa Romeo hardware. He won first time out, at Monaco, driving the Alfa Tipo B. Team-mate Achille Varzi closed the door in a tight finish at the Tripoli GP, leaving Moll fuming. He got his revenge at the Avusrennen three weeks later, beating Varzi into 2nd place. At the Coppa Acerbo at Pescara he was attempting to lap a back-marker when his Alfa, possibly hit by a cross-wind, left the track at 170 mph. Twenty-four-year-old Moll was dead by the time the car came to rest through trees some 400 metres away.

Juan Pablo Montoya

B. 20 SEPTEMBER 1975, BOGOTA, COLOMBIA

GRAND PRIX STARTS: 95

GRAND PRIX VICTORIES: 7

POINTS TOTAL: 307

Former CART champion and winner of the Indianapolis 500, Juan Pablo Montoya burst onto the F1 scene in 2001. He showed his brilliance time and again in his four seasons with Williams, though his combative nature produced the occasional costly error, particularly in the closely-fought 2003 championship.

Montoya first met Frank Williams at Silverstone in 1997, when he was competing in F3000. He signed on as test driver and also agreed a five-year option for his F1 services. After winning the F3000 title in 1998 the impetuous and impatient Montoya was disappointed not to be awarded a seat for 1999. Montoya finally got his chance in 2001. He took three poles that year, converting one of them, Monza, into a famous maiden victory. A year later, on the same track, Montoya broke Keke Rosberg's 17-year-old record for the fastest qualifying lap. His average 161.17 mph eclipsed the 160.397 set by the Finn at Silverstone in 1985. That season team-mate Ralf

Schumacher recorded Williams' sole success; but Montoya's seven poles was a clear indication that when it came to raw speed, he was as impressive as any man on the circuit.

Replaces Coulthard at McLaren

Montoya was on the podium seven times in 2002, finishing 3rd behind the all-conquering Ferrari duo. In 2003 he added two wins and nine podiums to his tally to get the better of Barrichello, only to finish behind Schumacher and Raikonnen in a tight title race. The gulf opened up again in 2004, Montoya slipping to 5th, almost 100 points adrift of the perennial champion. Long before the season was over it was announced that he would be replacing Coulthard at McLaren. His decision to link up with Raikonnen was seen as posing a formidable threat to Ferrari's five-year run of success.

2005 proved to be a mixed year for Montoya: early hopes thwarted by bad luck, interspersed with brilliant moments. Overcoming the unpredictability of his new McLaren, he took three wins and five podiums to finish 4th overall in the championship. He continued to drive for McLaren in 2006, but consistent underperformance put his future with the team in jeopardy.

A move to Nascar

The announcement that the reigning champion, Alonso, would join McLaren for the 2007 season made Montoya's future with the team more uncertain. Eventually he decided to call it a day and dropped out mid-season in favour of NASCAR racing.

Stirling Moss

B. 17 SEPTEMBER 1929, LONDON, ENGLAND

GRAND PRIX STARTS: 66

GRAND PRIX VICTORIES: 16 (1 SHARED)

POINTS TOTAL: 186.64

Widely regarded as the finest driver never to win the world title, Stirling Moss was nevertheless acclaimed as one of the greatest of his generation. Ultra-competitive and a consummate professional, Moss rapidly progressed through the junior ranks, making his F1 debut with HWM in 1951. Initially he struggled to make an impression on the Grand Prix circuit, driving British cars that were well off the pace compared with the dominant Italian marques.

In 1954 he ran a privately entered Maserati, and a fine 3rd at Spa helped secure a works drive before the season was out. Moss signed for Mercedes for 1955, scoring his maiden victory in the British Grand Prix. He finished runner-up to team-mate Fangio in the championship that year.

Wins home GP in Vanwall

It was the same first and second places for the next two seasons. In 1956 Moss rejoined Maserati and missed out on the title by three points. A year later, now with Vanwall, Moss scored three more victories, one of which came at the British GP. He took over Tony Brooks's car to claim his second home victory, but this time it was for a British outfit, a sweet moment for a great patriot. Three wins weren't enough to stop Fangio, who dominated in his Maserati that season.

1958 was the closest Moss came to winning the world crown. Despite four more victories, he lost out to compatriot Mike Hawthorn, who won just once. Moss crossed the line first in the title showdown race, the Moroccan GP, but Hawthorn's Ferrari eased through into 2nd to take the crown by a single point.

Moss gives Lotus first win

In 1959 Moss joined Rob Walker's outfit and again had a chance of winning the title going into the final race, the US GP. Mechanical failure meant he had to settle for 3rd in that season's championship. The following year the Walker team ran the new Lotus 18, and Moss gave the car its first victory, at Monaco. A crash during practice for Spa put him out for four rounds, and although he recovered to win the final race, he finished a distant 3rd behind Brabham and McLaren.

Goodwood crash ends career

Ferrari dominated in 1961, but Moss still won at Monaco and the Nurburgring, a superb effort in the underpowered Lotus. In 1962 Moss sustained appalling injuries in a non-championship race at Goodwood, ending his career in top-level motor sport. However, he had already done more than enough to establish himself as one of motor racing's legendary names, endearing himself to the British public in the process. His contribution to the sport was recognized with a knighthood, conferred on him in 2000.

Felice Nazzaro

B. 1880, TURIN, ITALY

D. 21 MARCH 1940

In a career spanning three decades, Felice Nazzaro showed himself to be a master of driving his cars just within the limit. While others crashed or pushed so hard that they suffered mechanical failure, Nazzaro invariably coaxed his car to the finish. This sometimes elicited the accusation that he inherited his wins; but in the era in which he was competing Nazzaro adopted not only a perfectly legitimate approach, but also the smartest.

Top driver of 1907

At the turn of the century Nazzaro was a Fiat apprentice, sent by the company to demonstrate the model which Sicilian customer Vicenzo

Florio had bought. The two became great friends, sharing a passion for racing. On one occasion Florio wanted to organize a race for his new motor tricycle, but as there was no motorized competition he organized a handicap event involving a cyclist and a horse. The horse won. In 1906 he oversaw the introduction of the famous Targa Florio, three daunting 92-mile laps over mountainous terrain. Nazzaro won the race the following year for Fiat. 1907 was Nazzaro's year: he also won the French GP and the newly inaugurated Kaiserpreis, a touring-car race staged on Germany's Taunus circuit.

Swansong victory has tragic turn

Nazzaro won the Targa Florio again in 1913, and in 1922 he claimed a second French GP victory, 15 years after his first. The veteran's last hurrah came in a Fiat 804 in a race staged at Strasbourg. It was a classic display from Nazzaro but one which had a tragic turn. A last-lap chase by his team-mates Pietro Bordini and Biagio Nazzaro resulted in a crash. Bordini survived but Nazzaro, Felice's nephew, was killed. The incident left Nazzaro running the sole Italian car to make it to the finish line, a typically measured performance for the wily campaigner.

Tazio Nuvolari

B. 18 November 1892, Mantua, Italy

D. 11 August 1953

The 'Flying Mantuan' is most people's choice as the pre-eminent racing driver of the pre-war period. He began his racing career on motorcycles, on one occasion competing with both legs in plaster casts after crashing in practice. He didn't turn seriously to four wheels until he was in his late thirties, but that didn't stop him from chalking up a string of GP victories. He also won all the other prestigious events on the calendar: the Targa Florio (1931 and 1932); the Mille Miglia (1930 and 1933); the Ards TT (1930 and 1933; and Le Mans (1933).

Shock victory in outdated Alfa

Famous for his animated driving style, Nuvolari joined Alfa Romeo's works team in 1932. The Tipo B P3, unveiled that year, was the first monoposto GP car, the regulations requiring two-seater bodywork having been scrapped. Nuvolari won numerous GPs over the next three years, though his greatest achievement came when the Alfa was outdated and the sleek German cars of the Mercedes and Auto Union stables were the best in the field. His victory at the 1935 German GP stunned the race organizers, who had the home national anthem cued up in expectation of victory. Nuvolari solved the problem by producing his own record of the Italian anthem.

'Death wish' bid fails

In 1938 Nuvolari signed for Auto Union, continuing his run of successes until GP racing was halted by the outbreak of war. He lost both of his sons in the conflict, and when he took to the track again many thought he was even more fearless than usual, intent on hastening his own demise. This was one of the few aims in which he was thwarted. His health deteriorated rapidly; his lungs had been damaged by many years of inhaling exhaust fumes, he began coughing up blood and then suffered a stroke which left him paralysed. Italy mourned when one of the country's great sporting heroes died, not on the track but in his bed, aged 61.

Olivier Panis

B. 2 SEPTEMBER 1966, LYON, FRANCE

GRAND PRIX STARTS: 158

GRAND PRIX VICTORIES: 1

POINTS TOTAL: 76

Olivier Panis signed off at Suzuka in 2004, having scored 12 points in his two seasons with Toyota, although he remained with the team for some time afterwards in the role of test driver.

Panis won the prestigious Volant Elf award at the famous Winfield racing school in 1987. Two years later he was the country's Formula Renault champion, and by 1991 he had completed two successful seasons in F3, finishing 4th and runner-up. Victory in the F3000 championship in 1993 brought him to the top division, Panis making his F1 debut with Ligier at Interlagos in 1994. His best result that year was second at Hockenheim, helped by a first-lap shunt which took out half the field. He also took 2nd in the 1994 decider at Adelaide, the final race to be staged there, though this time a spate of retirements aided his cause.

Maiden win from 14th on grid

At a wet Monaco in 1996 he started 14th on the grid but drove superbly to produce the upset of the year, holding off Coulthard's challenge to record his sole victory. It was Ligier's first success since Laffite's two wins in 1981.

Ligier evolved into Prost in 1997, and Panis immediately gave the new team its first points with 5th place in Melbourne. He followed it with a podium finish at Interlagos, scored at Monaco, then took 2nd behind Villeneuve's Williams in Spain. But in the next race, Montreal, he hit the barriers hard and broke both legs, curtailing a promising season.

Worsening relations at Prost

The 1998 Prost was a disappointment, and his relationship with the team worsened the following year. 2000 saw him as third-string at McLaren, where he was often as quick as Hakkinen and Coulthard in testing. Panis moved on to BAR, scoring just eight points in two seasons before using his experience to help Toyota mount an F1 challenge.

Riccardo Patrese

B. 17 APRIL 1954, PADUA, ITALY

GRAND PRIX STARTS: 256

GRAND PRIX VICTORIES: 6

POINTS TOTAL: 281

In 1974 Riccardo Patrese won the world karting championship, an achievement even the great Senna didn't manage. Two years later he lifted the European F3 title, and in 1977 made his F1 debut for Shadow, taking over from Renzo Zorzi. He scored his first championship point in the final race, the Japanese GP.

Banned after Monza crash

When members of the Shadow team left to form Arrows in 1978, Patrese went with them. He led for almost half the South African GP, and finished second to Lauda in Sweden, but encouraging results were blighted by the accident at Monza which resulted in Ronnie Peterson's death. He was barred from the next race at the behest of his fellow drivers, returning to take 4th in Montreal. Later investigations exonerated him from any blame for the Monza accident.

The next three seasons yielded a total of just 19 points, and in 1982 he moved to Brabham. It gave him his first win, at Monaco, although he was helped by the misfortune which struck Arnoux, Prost and Pironi. This was the year when victories were shared out, and just 23 points separated Patrese, in 10th, from champion Rosberg. A mistake cost him victory at Imola in 1983, and although he won the year's final race, he was very much the junior partner to Piquet, who took the crown.

Career reignited by Williams

After two disastrous years with Alfa Romeo, Patrese returned to a Brabham team on the slide. Williams reignited his career in 1988. After twice finishing 3rd, he was runner-up to Mansell in 1992. Second was his usual berth that year but he did win at Suzuka. His final victory came eleven years after his first, a F1 record. He retired after a swansong season with Benetton, this time playing the supporting role to Michael Schumacher. Riccardo Patrese's record of 256 races stood unbroken until Rubens Barichello overtook it in 2008.

Ronnie Peterson

B. 14 FEBRUARY 1944, OREBRO, SWEDEN

D. 11 SEPTEMBER 1978

GRAND PRIX STARTS: 123

GRAND PRIX VICTORIES: 10

POINTS TOTAL: 206

Although Ronnie Peterson was twice a world championship runner-up, his legions of fans felt that this did scant justice to a man they regarded as the most gifted driver of his era. He made his F1 debut in 1970, the year in which the sport mourned the loss of Jochen Rindt. Many felt that the Swede was Rindt's natural successor, just as Gilles Villeneuve took the mantle from Peterson.

Closest ever finish

It was his stunning performances in F3 and F2 which persuaded Max Mosley to sign him for the new March outfit in 1970. Promoted to the works team in 1971, Peterson took four 2nd places, one of which, Monza, provided the closest F1 finish ever. The Swede ended the race 0.01 seconds behind Peter Gethin's BRM, and fractionally ahead of Cevert and Hailwood. He ended the year as runner-up to Stewart.

After a disappointing 1972 Peterson switched to Lotus. He scored his maiden victory at Paul Ricard, and won in Austria after the team's no. 1 Fittipaldi, whom he had earlier waved through, retired from the race. Peterson had four victories in all to finish 3rd in the championship, though having been pole man nine times, improved reliability would have made it an even better year.

Leg injury complications

Peterson scored three more wins over the next two seasons in a Lotus which had fallen behind the competition. A win at Monza was the highlight of the 1976 season, back with March, and the following year he struggled with Tyrell's revolutionary P34 six-wheeler. 1978 saw him return to Lotus. Although he claimed two more wins, he played the supporting role to Mario Andretti. A crash at the start of the Italian GP left Peterson with serious leg injuries, and he died from complications the following day. He finished the year as posthumous runner-up in the championship.

Nelson Piquet

B. 17 FEBRUARY 1952, RIO DE JANEIRO, BRAZIL

GRAND PRIX STARTS: 204

GRAND PRIX VICTORIES: 23

POINTS TOTAL: 485.5

WORLD CHAMPION 1981, 1983, 1987

In 1987 Nelson Piquet became only the fifth man to win a hat-trick of world titles, a list of luminaries to which the names of Prost, Senna and Schumacher have since been added.

Brabham v Williams

Piquet made his F1 debut with Ensign at Hockenheim in 1978, then had three outings in a privately entered McLaren before joining Brabham for the final race of the season. He scored just three points in 1979. Team-mate Niki Lauda's departure left Piquet as the team's no. 1, and he pushed Alan Jones hard all the way in the 1980 championship. It was Brabham v Williams again in 1981. Piquet went into the final round, Las Vegas, trailing Reutemann by one point, but 5th place was enough to give him the crown, the Argentinian failing to score.

A switch to a BMW turbo unit was initially unsuccessful, but Piquet and Brabham roared back in 1983. It came to a last-race shoot-out with Prost, and Piquet clinched his second title with 3rd place at Kyalami.

Mansell injury hands title to Piquet

McLaren dominated the next two seasons, Piquet winning just three races in total. A switch to Williams in 1986 brought a dramatic climax, Piquet losing out in a three-way tussle with Prost and team-mate Mansell. The Williams pair again fought toe to toe in 1987, until an injury to Mansell in practice for the penultimate round, Suzuka, ended his season. Piquet didn't need to score to take his third title. After two indifferent years at Lotus Piquet ended his F1 career at Benetton, with whom he won the final three GPs of his career.

In 2007 Nelson Piquet Jr was appointed Renault test driver and promoted to a race seat alongside Fernando Alonso the following year. He scored his first points in his eighth race, the French GP, and was on the podium two rounds later at Hockenheim, where he finished second to Hamilton.

Alain Prost

b. 24 FEBRUARY 1955, ST CHAMOND, FRANCE

GRAND PRIX STARTS: 199

GRAND PRIX VICTORIES: 51

POINTS TOTAL: 798.5

WORLD CHAMPION 1985, 1986, 1989, 1993

Alain Prost became only the second man to win the world championship four times, following in Fangio's footsteps. Michael Schumacher has since joined that exclusive club, and has also overhauled Prost's tally of 51 wins, a record when he retired in 1993. Having started 199 Grands Prix, Prost topped the podium in one-quarter of the races in which he competed.

'The Professor'

Prost's hallmark was his cerebral approach to racing. F1 had had many dazzling speed merchants who were also car breakers; Prost husbanded his resources carefully, conserving tyres, brakes and fuel until exactly the right moment. His mastery of racing tactics earned him an apposite nickname: 'The Professor'.

The former world karting champion made his F1 debut in 1980 for McLaren, then a struggling outfit. The fact that Prost took a poor car to sixth place on his debut in Buenos Aires showed his enormous potential. That was confirmed with a move to Renault in 1981, Prost winning three races to finish fifth, just seven points behind champion Piquet. It was one place better the following year, despite a string of retirements, and his last season with Renault saw Piquet pip him for the title by two points.

Runner-up despite seven wins

Prost returned to McLaren, and although he won a remarkable seven

races in 1984 he again had to settle for the runner-up spot. Team-mate Niki Lauda, who won just five times, won the championship by finishing second to the Frenchman in the decider at Estoril. The margin was a wafer-thin half-point.

Five more wins brought Prost the 1985 championship with two races to spare. It would have been even more comfortable had he not had his Imola victory chalked off for an infringement of the weight regulations. He retained the title after getting the better of Williams pair Mansell and Piquet in a three-way showdown in Australia. Mansell's tyre blew, Piquet was brought in for a precautionary stop, leaving Prost to win both the race and the title.

Two Suzuka clashes with Senna

After a year of Williams domination, McLaren hit back in 1988, Prost and new team-mate Senna between them winning 15 of the 16 races. Prost outscored the Brazilian overall, but taking the best eleven results Senna had it by three points. The positions were reversed in 1989, their crash at Suzuka settling the championship in Prost's favour. It was another Senna–Prost show in 1990, and yet again the pair clashed at Suzuka, though this time it consigned the Frenchman to the runner-up spot. After a poor 1991 season Prost took a year's sabbatical. Williams brought him back in 1993 to replace reigning champion Mansell, and he added seven more victories to his tally to claim his fourth world crown.

Didier Pironi

B. 26 MARCH 1952, PARIS, FRANCE

D. 23 AUGUST 1987

GRAND PRIX STARTS: 70

GRAND PRIX VICTORIES: 3

POINTS TOTAL: 101

Didier Pironi, a graduate of the Winfield racing School, had a sparkling rise through the ranks in the mid-1970s. He finished behind team-mate René Arnoux and Eddie Cheever in the 1977 F2 championship, earning a F1 call up from talent-spotter supreme Ken Tyrell the following year. He finished 6th in the Brazilian GP, only his second race, and got into the points on four other occasions.

Pironi's second season with Tyrell saw him on the podium for the first time. He finished 3rd both at Zolder and Watkins Glen to finish on 14 points and 10th place – level with 1978 champion Mario Andretti.

Maiden win at Zolder

Ligier's Jacques Laffite and Patrick Depailler had both finished ahead of him, and the combination of a better car and a French team proved an irresistible attraction for 1980. Laffite ended the campaign with two more points, but he was almost a decade older; Pironi, who finished one place behind his team-mate in 5th, was one of the stars of the year. Zolder gave him his maiden victory, and with better luck he could have won twice more. He led at Monaco for 54 laps, only to clip a barrier; and at Brands Hatch, where he was again on pole, tyre problems cost him almost certain victory.

Defies team orders

Pironi took Scheckter's place at Ferrari in 1981, but was overshadowed by team-mate Gilles Villeneuve. Determined to make his mark in 1982, Pironi took victory against team orders at Imola, passing Villeneuve on the last lap. The latter was killed during qualifying for the next race, leaving Pironi as the focus of Ferrari attention. He won at Zandvoort, and by Round 12, Hockenheim, led by nine points. There he suffered career-ending leg injuries during practice. Even though he missed the last five races, he still finished runner-up, just five points behind Rosberg. Pironi took to racing powerboats, and was killed while competing off the Isle of Wight in 1987.

Kimi Räikkönen

B. 17 OCTOBER 1979, LAPPEENRANTA, FINLAND	
GRAND PRIX STARTS: 140*	
GRAND PRIX VICTORIES: 17*	
POINTS TOTAL: 531*	
WORLD CHAMPION 2007	
*TO END OF 2008 SEASON	

First there was Rosberg, then Hakkinen, and as the curtain was drawing down on the latter's illustrious career, Finland hailed the emergence of a new F1 star.

Kimi Räikkönen didn't turn to single-seaters until 1999. Seven wins in ten outings for Manor Motorsport in the 2000 British Formula Renault series was bound to attract the attention of bigger fish, and in September that year, he tested for Sauber. A few months later, with just 23 competitive races under his belt, he made his championship debut. His performance convinced Ron Dennis that he was the man to take over from compatriot Mika Hakkinen at McLaren.

Runs Schumacher close

In 2002 Räikkönen was the understudy, finishing the year in 6th, 17 points and one place behind David Coulthard. Within a year the Finn was not only McLaren's front-runner but also a title contender. Schumacher won six races, but finished the year just two points ahead of Räikkönen.

The 'Iceman' cometh

In 2004 Räikkönen scored a second win, at Spa, and notched 45 points. But early-season gremlins with the new car allowed Ferrari to pull away. Even so, in his four seasons in F1 the 'Iceman' has shown he has all the credentials to bring Schumacher's reign to an end.

2005 saw him emerge as a genuine championship contender. However, reliability problems, yet again, meant that he finished runner-up, 20 points adrift of Fernando Alonso. After wining no races and finishing 5th overall in 2006, Räikkönen made the switch from McLaren to Ferrari. Six wins helped him lift the 2007 title, pipping McLaren duo Hamilton and Alonso by a single point. He set the fastest lap in ten races in 2008, equalling Michael Schumacher's record and putting him third on the all-time list, but could finish only 3rd in the championship.

Carlos Reutemann

B. 12 APRIL 1942, SANTA FE, ARGENTINA
GRAND PRIX STARTS: 146
GRAND PRIX VICTORIES: 12
POINTS TOTAL: 310

Carlos Reutemann was one of F1's enigmas, possessing the talent to have gone to the very top, but just as likely to exasperate with a performance of abject mediocrity.

He travelled to Europe to compete in F2 in 1970, having won his home championship the previous year. His first campaign bore little fruit; his second ended in the runner-up spot, behind Ronnie Peterson.

In 1972 he signed for Bernie Ecclestone's Brabham team, taking a stunning pole on his debut, the Argentinian GP. However, he scored just three points that year, though team-mate and twice-world champion Graham Hill notched only four.

Typical rollercoaster season

A couple of podiums elevated Reutemann to 7th in the 1973 championship. The following year he led each of the first three races but won only one, Kyalami. In his home race he ran out of fuel with victory in sight. A dip in form, followed by further wins in Austria and the US, produced a typical rollercoaster season.

His Brabham career peaked with 3rd place in 1975, a season in which he won just once, in Germany, but was on the podium on five other occasions. After a disastrous 1976, down to Brabham's new Alfa Romeo engine, Reutemann had two years at Ferrari. In his first campaign he finished a distant 4th behind the team's star, Lauda, but he was top dog in 1978, scoring four wins to finish 3rd behind Lotus duo Andretti and Peterson. He then joined Andretti, but the new Lotus 80 underperformed badly.

Defeat snatched from jaws of victory

His final two campaigns were with Williams. In 1980 he backed up Alan Jones's title-winning season, and the roles should have been reversed the following season. He went into the final race, Caesar's Palace, a point clear of Piquet, but after taking pole he slumped to 8th. The Brazilian took 5th to snatch the crown by a point. Two races into the 1982 season Reutemann quit the sport.

Pedro Rodriguez

B. 18 JANUARY 1940, MEXICO CITY, MEXICO

D. 11 JULY 1971

GRAND PRIX STARTS: 55

GRAND PRIX VICTORIES: 2

POINTS TOTAL: 71

Pedro Rodriguez's younger brother Ricardo was considered to have more natural talent, but both were idolized at home as they established themselves in motor sport, initially in bike racing. Ricardo broke into F1 first, qualifying his Ferrari second on the grid on his debut, Monza '61. His death in the following year's non-championship Mexican GP left Pedro to make the family's mark on the world stage. Lotus gave him his first opportunity, at Watkins Glen in 1963. He retired that day, and in the following race in his native Mexico.

Works drive for Cooper

He made cameo appearances over the next three seasons: 6th in the 1964 Mexican GP, 7th in the same race a year later and 5th at Watkins Glen, all for Ferrari; in 1966 he was running strongly in a couple of outings for Lotus but failed to finish. In 1967 he finally got a full works drive, with Cooper. Although he missed three races through injury he won the South African GP to end the year in 6th place, well ahead of team-mate and future champion Jochen Rindt.

Rodriguez was 6th again in 1968, this time for BRM. Second to Bruce McLaren's DFV-powered car at Spa was his best result. He was a bit-part F1 player in 1969, starting the year in a privately entered BRM and ending it with Ferrari. He got into the points at Monza and Watkins Glen for Maranello, but for 1970 it was back to a full campaign with BRM.

First BRM win in four years

He gave the team its first victory in four years when he came out on top in a titanic duel with Chris Amon's March at Spa. He was also second to Fittipaldi in the US GP, finishing the year 7th in the championship.

1971 began promisingly, Rodriguez taking 2nd place behind Ickx's Ferrari at Zandvoort, and scoring in Spain. He was killed when his Ferrari crashed in a minor sports-car race at Norisring, Germany.

Jochen Rindt

B. 18 APRIL 1942, MAINZ-AM-RHEIN, GERMANY

D. 5 SEPTEMBER 1970

GRAND PRIX STARTS: 60

GRAND PRIX VICTORIES: 6

POINTS TOTAL: 109

WORLD CHAMPION 1970

As soon as Jochen Rindt swapped hill-climbs and rallies for circuit racing in the early 1960s his speed and style marked him out as a man to watch. He made his championship debut at Zeltweg in 1964, the first time that Austria had staged a title race. His Rob Walker Brabham failed to finish that day, but the following year saw him gain a berth alongside Bruce McLaren at Cooper. He scored his first championship points in 1965, but also competed in F2 races, and won at Le Mans.

Upward surge

The upward surge was relentless. Rindt was on the podium three times in 1966, and although he then struggled for a season, it was down to an uncompetitive Cooper, something confirmed by a string of wins in F2. The cars to beat were the Brabham-Repco and Lotus, which had just introduced the Cosworth DFV unit. Rindt would have spells with both teams. The season with Brabham didn't go well. The team that had produced the world champion for two seasons chose this year to suffer reliability problems and a dramatic slump in fortunes. Rindt moved to Lotus in 1969, joining reigning champion Graham Hill. He outscored Hill in a season which produced his maiden victory, at Watkins Glen.

First posthumous champion

Hill was badly injured at the 1969 US GP, and although he was back on the grid for 1970, he would never recover his form. Fittipaldi was drafted in, but Rindt was Lotus's main man. He rose to the challenge superbly, winning five races out of six in mid-season to lead the title race comfortably. Rindt was killed during practice for Monza. There were still four races to go but Ferrari's Jacky Ickx, the only man who could catch him, was unable to bridge the gap. Rindt thus became the first posthumous world champion.

Keke Rosberg

B. 6 DECEMBER 1948, STOCKHOLM, SWEDEN

GRAND PRIX STARTS: 114

GRAND PRIX VICTORIES: 5

POINTS TOTAL: 159.5

WORLD CHAMPION 1982

The 'Flying Finn' spent four seasons with unheralded teams in the F1 basement, scoring an aggregate of just six points between 1978 and 1981. It was thus an inspired decision on the part of Williams to choose Rosberg as the man to replace Alan Jones in 1982, one which was vindicated as he reclaimed the crown that the team had lost to Piquet and Brabham the previous year.

Replaces Hunt at Wolf

Rosberg struggled to qualify his Theodore in the 1978 F1 series, though he drove the car to an outstanding victory in the International Trophy at a rain-soaked Silverstone. He had a few outings for ATS, and also returned to Theodore, this time running a Wolf. Nor did he make much impact in 1979, when he took over from James Hunt at Wolf. By 1980 Walter Wolf had had enough and the team merged with Fittipaldi, and Rosberg found himself partnering the 1972 and 1974 world champion. Third place in Buenos Aires helped the Finn to outscore Fittipaldi, albeit by a single point. Fittipaldi moved upstairs in 1981, Rosberg being joined by Chico Serra. Once again the battle was in qualifying rather than trying to get into the points.

Ten scoring finishes

In 1982 Rosberg was handed his big chance, the first time he had competitive hardware, and he grabbed it with both hands. He received a further boost when Reutemann quit after two races and he was elevated to team leader. Rosberg won only once, the Swiss GP, but was consistently in the points, scoring ten times in a season when the best eleven finishes counted. He held off the challenge of John Watson to secure the title with 5th place at Caesar's Palace.

Rosberg won twice in the next two seasons, hampered by the late arrival of the Williams turbo unit, and then struggling to come to terms with it. He finished 3rd in the 1985 championship, but slipped to 6th the following season with McLaren, his swansong F1 campaign.

Nico Rosberg

B. 27 JUNE 1985, WIESBADEN, GERMANY

GRAND PRIX STARTS: 53*

GRAND PRIX VICTORIES: 0

POINTS TOTAL: 41*

*TO END OF 2008 SEASON

The son of the 1982 champion, Finland's Keke Rosberg, Nico was born in Wiesbaden and holds dual nationality, though he races under a German flag.

Formula BMW champion

Rosberg took up karting at the age of 11, and just six years later, in 2002, won the inaugural German Formula BMW championship. He competed in the Formula Three Euroseries for his father's team in 2003 and 2004, finishing 8th and 4th respectively. He had already tested for Williams, and after an outstanding 2005, when he won the inaugural GP2 championship for the ART Grand Prix team, he joined the Grove-based outfit, replacing BMW Sauber-bound Nick Heidfeld. Williams had seven drivers' championships and nine constructors' titles to its name, but the last of those had come in 1997, so it was always going to be a testing F1 baptism for 20-year-old Rosberg.

A promising F1 debut

There was a highly promising start as he and partner Mark Webber both got into the points at the Bahrain curtain-raiser. Rosberg immediately went into the record books, taking over from Fernando Alonso as the youngest driver to set the fastest lap in a grand prix. The rest of the season was something of an anti-climax, Rosberg and Webber between them suffering 20 retirements. Rosberg's only other scoring race was the European GP, where he again took 7th place.

First podium finish

Williams adopted Toyota power in 2007, and Rosberg's fortunes took a turn for the better. He was among the points in seven races, a fine late-season run culminating in 4th place at Interlagos. He couldn't quite improve on his 20-point haul the following season, but 2008 did see Rosberg on the podium for the first time. He finished 3rd in the season-opener in Melbourne, and went one better in F1's first ever floodlit race around the streets of Singapore.

Bernd Rosemeyer

B. 14 OCTOBER 1909, LINGEN, GERMANY

D. 28 JANUARY 1938

In a short, stellar career, Bernd Rosemeyer rose to the pinnacle of motor sport and became a national hero and an icon to all racing enthusiasts. He started out on bikes, and his talent on two wheels brought an offer to join DKW in 1934. DKW was part of the newly formed Auto Union, and a year later the umbrella group chose Rosemeyer to drive the Ferdinand Porsche-designed 16-cylinder car in the premier racing class. He turned up for the Nurburgring trial wearing a suit instead of overalls, since this was a red-letter day. It was a steep learning curve, and there was the odd accident, but the gifted Rosemeyer was soon matching the times of vastly more experienced drivers.

European champion in first full season

Before the year was out he had claimed his first victory, at the Czech GP, finishing six minutes ahead of Nuvolari. 1936 – his first full campaign – saw Rosemeyer become European champion, then the most prestigious title in motor racing. He won the German, Pescara, Swiss and Italian GPs, though his greatest victory came at the Eifelrennen, staged at the Nurburgring. After a titanic struggle with Rudi Caracciola in near-impenetrable mist, the triumphant Rosemeyer earned the tag 'Nebelmeister' – Fogmaster.

Political pawn

By the end of 1937 Rosemeyer had notched ten victories from 31 starts in GP-class races. He was used for propaganda purposes by the National Socialists, who portrayed him as the archetypal Aryan. Politics also played a part in his death. The Nazis were keen to use the world speed record as a symbol of German supremacy, and both Auto Union and rivals Mercedes were encouraged to outdo each other. Rosemeyer set a new mark in October 1937, the first man to break the 250-mph barrier. Mercedes' Caracciola raised the bar to 268 mph in January the following year, on a stretch of autobahn near Frankfurt. Rosemeyer was killed during his attempt to recapture the record, hurled out of his car at 270 mph.

Jody Scheckter

B. 29 JANUARY 1950, EAST LONDON, SOUTH AFRICA

GRAND PRIX STARTS: 112

GRAND PRIX VICTORIES: 10

POINTS TOTAL: 255

WORLD CHAMPION 1979

Jody Scheckter was initially seen as scintillatingly quick but something of a liability. Before he made his F1 debut in 1972 he had had countless spins, and he did his reputation no good by initiating a monster 20-car pile-up at Silverstone in the first lap of the 1973 British GP. His McLaren had been 4th at the time, and he had led the previous race, Paul Ricard, for 41 of the 54 laps. If McLaren saw the negative side, Ken Tyrell recognized the huge potential, signing him in 1974 to replace the retired Jackie Stewart.

Gives six-wheeler its only victory

Victories in Sweden and Britain, plus a couple of 2nd places put him in with an outside chance of the title, but he failed to score in the decider, Watkins Glen, and had to settle for 3rd behind Fittipaldi and Regazzoni. Success in his home GP was the highlight of 1975, when he slipped to 7th in the overall rankings. Tyrell then unveiled its six-wheeled P34. Scheckter drove it to 2nd place in only its third outing, Monaco, then went one better at Anderstorp. It would be the car's sole success.

In 1977 Scheckter gave another car its only taste of victory. He joined the new Wolf team, won first time out in the WR1 in Buenos Aires, and also crossed the line first in Monaco and Canada. Scheckter stayed in contention with Lauda's Ferrari for most of the year but had to content himself with runner-up to the Austrian.

Consistency proves key to title win

After a disappointing second season with Wolf, Scheckter joined Ferrari. Reliability proved key, and three wins plus a string of points finishes helped the South African take the title from team-mate Villeneuve, who was under orders to play the supporting role. The 1980 car, by contrast, was a disaster, Scheckter picking up just two points all year. He retired at the end of that campaign.

Ralf Schumacher

B. 30 JUNE 1975, HURTH-HERMUTHLHEIM, GERMANY	
GRAND PRIX STARTS: 180	
GRAND PRIX VICTORIES: 6	
POINTS TOTAL: 329	

Ralf Schumacher emerged from his brother's shadow in 1999, his third year in F1 and first with Williams. Ralf Schumacher emerged as a hard charger, scoring in all but one of the races where he went the distance. With better luck he might have won the Italian and European Grands Prix.

Schumacher rose to prominence in the German F3 championship of 1994. Third that season, runner-up the next, he and manager Willy Weber then decided Formula Nippon was the next move. Ralf won the title at the first attempt, though McLaren, for whom he tested in 1996, were less enthusiastic.

Jordan's tyros

Jordan stepped in to offer Schumacher his F1 break in 1997. He garnered just 14 points from his second season, alongside Damon Hill, then left to join Williams. While Schumacher grew in stature, team-mate Alex Zanardi fell by the wayside. Ralf got on the podium at Melbourne, his Willliams debut, from 8th on the grid.

Ends Williams' barren run

At Imola in 2001 he scored his maiden win, ending a 54-race barren run for the team. At Montreal he led Michael home, as they became the first siblings to finish 1-2 in a championship race. His third win in 2001 came at Hockenheim, the first time a German had won in German-engined car since Caracciola's Mercedes in 1939.

Three wins in the next two years put him 4th and 5th in the championship, each time outscored by team-mate Montoya. After slipping to 9th in 2004 Schumacher took up a new challenge by joining Toyota. For the first 12 races of 2005, he was outraced by team-mate Jarno Trulli, but showed some promise towards the end, taking a third at the Chinese GP. He ended the season sixth overall, 2 points ahead of Trulli.

A new challenge

Having totalled just 25 points in the 2006 and 2007 seasons, Schumacher quit F1 to compete in the German touring car series.

Michael Schumacher

B. 3 JANUARY 1969, HURTH-HERMUHLHEIM, GERMANY

GRAND PRIX STARTS: 248

GRAND PRIX VICTORIES: 91

POINTS TOTAL: 1369

WORLD CHAMPION
1994, 1995, 2000, 2001, 2002, 2003, 2004

Schumacher, in a league of his own, has rewritten the record books. He is the only driver to have taken five championships in a row, surpassing Fangio.

Inauspicious debut

Schumacher's F1 debut came at Spa in 1991, driving for Jordan. He retired before the end of the first lap, but in qualifying 7th he'd already proved that he had talent. Benetton quickly signed him and he rewarded them with a 5th at Monza two weeks later. In his first full season in 1992, he was regularly on the podium, and this, together with a maiden win at Spa, put him 3rd in the championship that year. 1993 gave him another win, plus eight podiums.

Consecutive titles

1994 saw him take his first title, albeit after a controversial collision involving championship rival Damon Hill in the showdown race at Adelaide. He retained the title in 1995 with nine wins, casting aside all doubts as to his championship abilities.

Dominant at Ferrari

In 1996, he moved to Ferrari, whose car was not as fast as Williams, and suffered a temporary setback. He began his dominance of F1 in 2000, taking five consecutive championship titles, his best year being 2004 when he won 12 of the first 13 rounds. At the beginning of 2005, rule changes were introduced by the FIA to try to level the playing field and make the racing more competitive. Whether as a result of this or not, Schumacher had a disappointing season, taking just one victory – at Indianapolis – and making five podiums. He finished the season third behind Alonso and Räikkönen.

Final season

2006 was to be Schumacher's final season in Formula One and his chances of winning one last championship were slim with Alonso dominating at the beginning of the season. However, in a thrilling reversal of fortunes, Schumacher began to catch up and eventually he and Alonso were neck and neck with just two races to go. Sadly, engine trouble forced Schumacher out of the penultimate race in Japan, which pushed Alonso too far out of his grasp. He may have finished his last championship in second position, but his place among the sports all-time greats had been assured long before.

Henry Segrave

B. BALTIMORE, USA, 1896

D. 13 JUNE 1930

Henry Segrave's short life read like a *Boy's Own* story. He was a celebrated war hero who turned his attention to motor sport after he was demobbed, excelling both on the track and in his famous speed record attempts on land and water. A three-time winner of the Junior Car Club 200 Mile race at Brooklands, Segrave made history by winning the 1923 French GP. It was the first victory for a British driver in a British car, a feat that would remain unequalled for more than 30 years. He followed it up by winning the Spanish GP the following year, and set a fastest lap of 85.99 mph at the inaugural British GP, staged at Brooklands in 1926, before a supercharger problem put him out of the race.

First man to break 200 mph barrier

Thereafter speed records increasingly began to occupy his thoughts. In March 1927 he took *Mystery Sunbeam* to 203.79 mph at Daytona, becoming the first man to break the 200 mph barrier. Two years later he set a new mark of 231.446 mph in *Golden Arrow*. The car was mothballed with just 18.74 miles on the clock, one of the least used vehicles in motoring history.

Killed during attempt on water speed record

Segrave then turned his attention to the water speed record. In 1930 he went to Lake Windermere with his boat *Miss England II* to try to capture the record, which then stood at 92.83 mph. He reached over 96 mph on his first run but crashed on the return. He died later from his injuries, along with another member of the three-strong crew. The Segrave Trophy was inaugurated that same year, an annual award given to the Briton who had achieved the most notable feat on land, sea or air in that period.

Raymond Sommer

B. 31 AUGUST 1906, MOUZON, FRANCE

D. 10 SEPTEMBER 1950

Had Raymond Sommer driven for Mercedes in his 1930s heyday, he would undoubtedly have had an even more impressive curriculum vitae. But Sommer eschewed the constraints that would have accompanied being tied to the major teams. On the occasions when he was affiliated to a works outfit, Sommer insisted on retaining privateer status. He relished the challenge of taking on the latest hardware in outdated machinery. The French public appreciated his talent and commitment, dubbing him 'Coeur de Lion'.

Drove 20 hours at Le Mans

Sommer's approach meant that his greatest successes came in sports car races. He won at Le Mans in 1932 and 1933, partnered by Luigi Chinetti and Tazio Nuvolari respectively. In the former race Chinetti fell ill and Sommer drove for 20 of the 24 hours. His victory in the 1936 French GP at Montlhery was helped by the fact that the organizers held it as a sports-car race, a decision aimed at derailing the dominant German marques. He and Wimille shared victory in a Bugatti, and in the same season Sommer won the Spa 24-Hour race.

Alfa team stunned

Sommer was named French champion in 1937 and 1939, and would have been in his prime during the war years. In 1946 he drove a Maserati to a stunning victory over the 158 Alfettas at St Cloud, beating the car which would dominate the inaugural world championship. He was recruited to drive the state-backed CTA-Arsenal at the 1947 French GP. The car didn't make it across the start line, though the fiasco failed to dent Sommer's reputation.

He scored a fine 4th place at the 1950 Monaco GP, driving a F2 Ferrari. At Spa the Alfa team was so shocked when Sommer's Lago-Talbot was recorded as race leader that they checked with the timekeepers to ensure they hadn't miscalculated. In September, having just been awarded the Légion d'Honneur, Sommer was killed while driving a Cooper in a minor race at Cadours.

Ayrton Senna

B. 21 MARCH 1960, SÃO PAULO, BRAZIL

D. 1 MAY 1994

GRAND PRIX STARTS: 161

GRAND PRIX VICTORIES: 41

POINTS TOTAL: 614

WORLD CHAMPION 1988, 1990, 1991

To many F1 aficionados Ayrton Senna was, quite simply, the greatest of them all. Sixty-five pole positions, 41 wins, 80 times in all on the podium, 614 points; the statistics are staggering, whichever way you consider them.

Senna won a host of karting titles – though just missed out on the world championship – before moving to Britain to further his career in four-wheeled competition. Within three years he had won the British F3 title, holding off the challenge of Martin Brundle. The following season, 1984, he made his F1 debut. Senna had tested for Brabham and Williams, between them winners of the previous four world championships, but he chose to join the unheralded Toleman team.

First victories with Lotus
He scored his first point at Kyalami, and in his sixth outing, Monaco, he was lying 2nd and running Prost hard when the race was red-flagged. Before the season was out he'd signed for Lotus, with whom he scored his first wins, Estoril and Spa, in '85. The ruthless streak which caused him to leave Toleman came to the fore when he vetoed the arrival of Derek Warwick at Lotus; Senna wanted no threat to his no. 1 status.

Rivals and team-mates

Six wins in three years at Lotus had elevated him to 4th, 3rd and 3rd in the championship. That was never going to be enough, and Senna joined McLaren in 1988. Prost had already been there four years, winning the title twice. They were team-mates and bitter rivals for two seasons. In 1988 Senna took eight wins, Prost seven, and the Brazilian won his first championship by three points. The following season there were six more wins, but Prost relegated him to runner-up spot after their famous clash at Suzuka. Prost departed for Ferrari but it was deja-vu as another spat in Japan settled the 1990 championship, this time in Senna's favour. Initially he protested his innocence; later he admitted guilt.

Killed in third race for Williams

He claimed his third title by a comfortable 24-point margin over Mansell, but Williams was on the up. It was a fine effort to win three Grands Prix in 1992, a year dominated by the FW14B. In 1993 Senna was not only up against Williams, who now boasted Prost as no. 1, but hampered by the loss of the Honda engine, the McLaren now running an indifferent Ford V8 unit. Five wins earned him only the runner-up spot, though it could be argued it was his greatest year.

Senna joined Williams in 1994. He took pole in the first two rounds but retired in each. He was on pole again at Imola, when he crashed fatally at Tamburello.

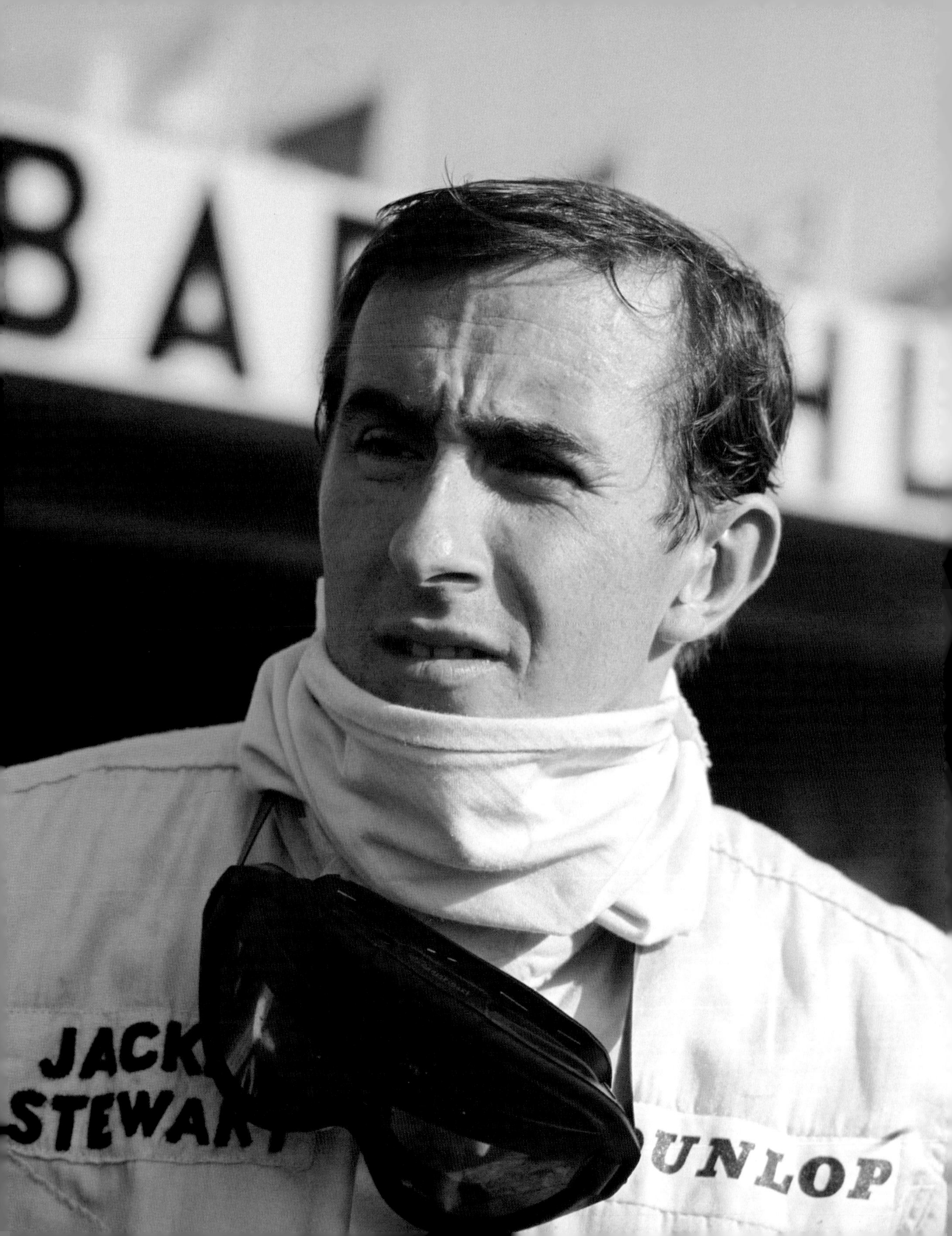
JACK
STEWAR
UNLOP

Jackie Stewart

B. 11 JUNE 1939, MILTON, SCOTLAND

GRAND PRIX STARTS: 99

GRAND PRIX VICTORIES: 27

POINTS TOTAL: 360

WORLD CHAMPION 1969, 1971, 1973

Jackie Stewart was a member of the British clay-pigeon shooting team in the late 1950s, just missing out on a place at the 1960 Olympic Games. That bitter disappointment spurred him on to scale great heights when he turned his attention to motor racing, following in his older brother's footsteps. Stewart was a natural behind the wheel, and it wasn't long before his talent attracted the attention of some of the sport's major players.

F1 debut with BRM
Ken Tyrell stole a march, signing Stewart for his F3 team in 1964. He continued to impress and, with several teams keen to offer him a F1 contract, he opted to sign for BRM.

His championship debut came at the curtain-raiser to the 1965 season, the South African GP. A fine 6th place that day was followed by a string of terrific performances, culminating in a maiden victory at Monza. It was a stunning debut season, Stewart finishing 3rd behind one of his heroes, Jim Clark, and team-mate Graham Hill.

Safety campaigner
Stewart remained at BRM for two more years, but the car was both uncompetitive and unreliable and results were indifferent. He won just once in that time, the 1966 Monaco GP. In that year's race at Spa he was involved in a huge first-lap pile-up, following which he became a leading light in the campaign to improve safety in F1.

In 1968 Stewart was reunited with Tyrell, the beginning of a long and glorious partnership that would yield three world titles. Injury forced him to miss two races in 1968, when he finished runner-up to Hill. The following season he and the Matra MS80 annihilated the opposition. Six wins put him 26 points clear of Jacky Ickx in the final table.

Six wins bring second title
There was a disappointing hiatus in 1970 as the team ran a March chassis which underperformed compared to the Matra. Tyrell began work on his own car, which was unveiled late in the 1970 campaign. Stewart romped to his second world title in 1971, winning six of the eleven rounds. There were four more victories in 1972, but Lotus's Emerson Fittipaldi went one better and Stewart, suffering from a stomach ulcer, had to settle for the runner-up spot. The positions were reversed the following year, Stewart adding five more victories to his tally. With his third championship already in the bag, Stewart planned to bow out at the US GP, which would have been his 100th race. But the death of team-mate Francois Cevert during qualifying prompted Tyrell to withdraw and Stewart to retire with immediate effect. His 27 wins set a new world mark that was to stand for 14 years.

John Surtees

B. 11 FEBRUARY 1934, TATSFIELD, ENGLAND	
GRAND PRIX STARTS: 111	
GRAND PRIX VICTORIES: 6	
POINTS TOTAL: 180	
WORLD CHAMPION 1964	

John Surtees remains the only man to have won world championships on both two wheels and four. Motorcycling was in the blood, Surtees' father owning a bike shop and competing at a modest level. John landed his first world title in 1956 and followed it up with six more championships over the next three years, winning both the 350cc and 500cc classes.

In 1960 Surtees was offered a F1 drive with Lotus, initially fitting GP racing round his motorcycling schedule. In only his second outing, at Silverstone, he finished 2nd to reigning champion Jack Brabham.

Ferrari overture rejected

Surtees left to join Yeoman Credit Cooper, unhappy with the political wrangling over the driver line-up at Lotus. 1961 yielded just four championship points, but that reflected the quality of the car, not the driver. Surtees declined an offer from Ferrari, choosing to remain with the team which was now running Lolas under the Bowmaker banner. He finished 4th in the 1962 championship, and, after further overtures from Ferrari, this time he felt that the time was right.

It was 4th again in 1963, the season yielding Surtees' first victory, at the Nurburgring. Two more wins in 1964 meant that the final race, the Mexican GP, was a three-way title showdown, Hill and Clark also in contention. Luck went with Surtees as both rivals hit trouble, and his team-mate Lorenzo Bandini allowed him through to take 2nd place, enough to win the championship by a single point.

Rift with Maranello

1965 was blighted by engine-development problems and severe injuries sustained in a CanAm sports-car race. A rift with Ferrari saw Surtees join Cooper during the 1966 season, in which he finished runner-up. After two years helping Honda to establish itself in F1, and a disappointing year with BRM, Surtees formed his own team. In 1972 he retired from GP racing, to concentrate on management, but results were indifferent and the team folded in 1978.

Jarno Trulli

B. 13 JULY 1974, PESCARA, ITALY

GRAND PRIX STARTS: 202*

GRAND PRIX VICTORIES: 1*

POINTS TOTAL: 214*

*TO END OF 2008 SEASON

Jarno Trulli came from a family of motor sport fans and was named after a Finnish motorcycle racer, which caused confusion in media circles when he began to make a name for himself on four wheels. He won a string of karting titles, including the world crown, before switching to compete in the German F3 championship in 1996, where he was also victorious.

F1 debut with Minardi

Trulli made his F1 debut with Minardi the following year, joining the Prost team mid-season as replacement for the injured Olivier Panis. He scored his first championship points at the Nurburgring, and led the Austrian GP for 37 laps before his engine gave out. Such performances earned him a seat alongside Panis for the next two seasons, but points were hard to come by for the fledgling French outfit, and his best return was second place in an attritional 1999 European GP.

Maiden victory at Monaco

There followed a two-year spell at Jordan, a period in which he struggled to turn solid qualifying performances into points. Even when he got onto the front row, luck never seemed to favour him and 4th was his best showing. Trulli joined the new Renault F1 team in 2002, and although his first season suggested he had gained little from the move, things looked up considerably thereafter. The 2003 package was much more competitive and he scored another podium success at Hockenheim on his way to 33 points and 8th place, comfortably his best effort thus far. 2004 began even better. He was regularly in the points, and registered his maiden victory from pole at Monaco.

A seat with Toyota

Things went downhill soon after, and relations with team boss Flavio Briatore soured. Renault ousted him to make room for Jacques Villeneuve and Trulli signed for Toyota. He got a couple of late-season drives for his new team following Panis's retirement, and gave Toyota its first pole at Indianapolis in 2005, the race famous for the withdrawal of the Michelin-shod teams, including Toyota. He got onto the podium three times that year, nine scoring finishes bringing him 43 points and 7th place in the championship. Toyota found it difficult to break out of the midfield ranks, however, and when Trulli took 3rd at Magny-Cours in 2008, it was the team's first podium finish in over two years.

Achille Varzi

B. 8 AUGUST 1904, GALLIATE, ITALY

D. 1 JULY 1948

Achille Varzi's rivalry with Tazio Nuvolari was one of the highlights of the motor racing scene in the 1930s. Both were accomplished motorcycle racers – Varzi won several Italian titles – and the two were briefly team-mates, when Nuvolari acquired a pair of Bugattis in 1928. Their paths soon diverged, however. Varzi, who came from a wealthy family, was able to buy himself an Alfa Romeo P2, and his success with that car prompted Nuvolari to acquire an identical model.

Breaks Bugatti stranglehold

In 1930 Varzi endeared himself to Italian fans by winning the Targa Florio, breaking a five-year run of successes for Bugatti. In that race he came out on top in a great battle with Louis Chiron, but the following year the two were partners in the French GP, winning the ten-hour, 782-mile race in a Bugatti T51. Varzi also drove the T51 to victory in the 1931 Monaco GP, the first in which grid positions were determined by practice times.

The 1933 Monaco GP was an extraordinary tussle between Varzi and Nuvolari. The two traded the lead for virtually the entire 100 laps before a mechanic intervened to help push Nuvolari's ailing car, earning the Flying Mantuan a disqualification.

Morphia addiction

After winning nine races for Alfa in 1934, and also the Mille Miglia, Varzi signed for Auto Union. There were more victories – he would win 28 major races in all – but by 1936 his career had begun to wane. He had health problems, became addicted to morphia, and also began to be overshadowed by rising star Rosemeyer.

Varzi made a very successful surprise comeback in the early postwar period, but was killed during practice for the 1948 Swiss GP at Bremgarten. It was only the second accident of his long and illustrious career.

Sebastian Vettel

B. 4 MARCH 1972, MONFORT, HOLLAND

GRAND PRIX STARTS: 26*

GRAND PRIX VICTORIES: 1*

POINTS TOTAL: 41*

*TO END OF 2008 SEASON

Lewis Hamilton took the accolades for becoming the youngest ever world champion in 2008, but he was not the only record-breaker among the young bloods that year. It was easy to overlook the enormous strides made by Sebastian Vettel, in his first full season in the elite division.

Karting star

Vettel was a junior karting star who swept the board when he stepped up to the German Formula BMW Championship in 2004. He locked horns with Hamilton in the Formula 3 Euroseries in 2005, finishing 5th that year and runner-up the next. He went into 2007 as BMW Sauber test driver, while also competing in the Renault World Series. Vettel made his F1 debut at the US Grand Prix, replacing the injured Robert Kubica. Fellow test driver Timo Glock had had a spell with Jordan in 2004, but the team's decision was vindicated as the 19-year-old finished in 8th place, taking over from Jenson Button as the youngest driver to score a championship point.

Youngest race winner

Vettel was contracted to Red Bull from the end of 2007, but BMW Sauber released him early so that he could join Red Bull's sister outfit Scuderia Toro Rosso, who had lost Scott Speed. He finished 4th in Shanghai in the penultimate race of the year, but it was in 2008 when he really began to show his mettle. He scored in seven of the last nine races, including a maiden victory from pole at Monza. With that success he displaced Fernando Alonso as F1's youngest race winner.

A place with Toro Rosso's sister team

Vettel finished 8th in the championship with a highly creditable 35 points, and it was no surprise when he was named in the Red Bull line-up for 2009, replacing David Coulthard.

Gilles Villeneuve

B. 18 JANUARY 1950, ST-JEAN-SUR-RICHELIEU, CANADA
D. 8 MAY 1982
GRAND PRIX STARTS: 67
GRAND PRIX VICTORIES: 6
POINTS TOTAL: 107

Regarded as one of the most mercurial talents ever to grace F1, Gilles Villeneuve was a snowmobile champion who used his success in that sport to fund his early foray into four-wheeled competition with Formula Ford. In 1976 he won an invitation race which included reigning champion James Hunt, and a year later he retained his Canadian Formula Atlantic title.

McLaren gave Villeneuve his F1 debut at the 1977 British GP, and although he finished 11th behind race winner and team-mate Hunt, the latter had the new M26 model, Villeneuve competing superbly in the ageing M23. Incredibly, McLaren chose to dispense with his services, and before the season was out he was driving for Ferrari, replacing Lauda. He would remain at Maranello for the rest of his brief but scintillating career.

Victim of team orders

Villeneuve scored his maiden victory on home soil in the final round of the 1978 championship. A year later he twice led new team-mate Jody Scheckter home, at Kyalami and Long Beach, and added a third victory in the final race at Watkins Glen. Scheckter already had the title sewn up by then, Villeneuve having to fall in line with team orders. He finished runner-up to the South African in the championship.

Spat with Pironi

The 1980 Ferrari was a disaster: Villeneuve scored only six points, while the reigning world champion had just one 5th place and two points to show for his efforts. The 1981 model wasn't much better, but it had a new V6 turbo unit and Villeneuve won in Monaco and Spain to lead the Ferrari fight and finish 7th overall.

At the 1982 San Marino GP Villeneuve was left seething after team-mate Didier Pironi passed him on the last lap, breaking an agreement. Qualifying for the next race, at Zolder, took place in an air of simmering resentment. Villeneuve, desperate to grab pole, struck Jochen Mass's March and was hurled from his Ferrari and killed.

Jacques Villeneuve

---

b. 9 April 1971, St Jean-sur-Richelieu, Canada

Grand Prix starts: 165

Grand Prix victories: 11

Points total: 235

World Champion 1997

Villeneuve's period in the doldrums followed a meteoric rise to become world champion, something his illustrious father never managed. In 1995 he became the youngest ever winner of the Indy Car championship, taking time out to test for Williams and secure a two-year deal. An oil leak prevented him from a maiden victory on his debut, Melbourne 1996. He had to wait just three races, winning the European GP at the Nurburgring by beating Schumacher's Ferrari in a dash for the line. Three more wins followed, and he emerged as the only rival to team-mate Damon Hill. His slim chance ended when he crashed out at Suzuka, Hill winning when he needed just one point.

Schumacher's desperate tactics

The title came at the second attempt. There were seven wins, and a dramatic showdown at Jerez, the final round. Schumacher, leading the title race by a point, attempted to shunt his rival out of the race. Villeneuve recovered to finish 3rd and take the crown.

After just two podiums in 1998, Villeneuve began his five-year stint at BAR. The team didn't register a single point in 1999, the next four years produced an aggregate 40 points, and at the end of 2003 BAR dispensed with his services. He had three blank outings for Renault at the end of the 2004 season before joining Sauber. The 2005 Championship saw Villeneuve score just nine points but he continued to race for the newly-named BMW Sauber team in 2006. However, a crash in the German GP left him with injuries, which forced his team to bring in a replacement, Robert Kubica. Villeneuve was being edged out of the team as Kubica put in several impressive performances, finishing on the podium in only his third race. As a result the former champion decided to retire from the sport during the middle of the season.

Wolfgang von Trips

B. 4 MAY 1928, COLOGNE, GERMANY

D. 10 SEPTEMBER 1961

GRAND PRIX STARTS: 27

GRAND PRIX VICTORIES: 2

POINTS TOTAL: 56

Germany was on the verge of acclaiming Wolfgang von Trips as its first world champion when tragedy struck at the penultimate race of the 1961 season. His Ferrari team-mate Phil Hill took the title by one point, and German fans had to wait 33 years before a certain Michael Schumacher lifted the first of his championships.

Promoted to Ferrari team

Von Trips was a member of Ferrari's sports car team in 1956, gaining promotion to the F1 team for the Italian GP. An accident during practice delayed his debut, which took place in Buenos Aires, the curtain-raiser to the 1957 season. He finished 6th that day, and got onto the podium at Monza. Ferrari lost both Castellotti and de Portago that year, and von Trips was awarded a full-time seat for 1958. He and Phil Hill each scored a respectable 9 points, playing the junior role to Hawthorn and Collins. But while Hill was retained, von Trips was released at the end of the year, and he spent most of the 1959 season driving for Porsche in F2. However, he was back in the Scuderia fold for the final championship race, the team having lost the services of Jean Behra.

First postwar win for Germany

1960 saw Ferrari struggle against the dominant rear-engined opposition, Maranello holding out for one more campaign in the front-engined D246. In such circumstances 6th place, just behind Hill, was a valiant effort. By contrast, Ferrari had the car to beat in 1961, the superb 'sharknose' the best in the field as the new 1.5-litre formula arrived. At Zandvoort he became the first German to win a postwar GP. Victory at Aintree and two 2nd places put him in line for the title when the circus went to Monza. Von Trips, on pole, clashed with Jim Clark's Lotus on the first lap. He was killed, along with a dozen spectators.

Mark Webber

B. 27 AUGUST 1976, QUEANBEYAN, AUSTRALIA

GRAND PRIX STARTS: 123*

GRAND PRIX VICTORIES: 0*

POINTS TOTAL: 100*

*TO END OF 2008 SEASON

The son of a New South Wales motorcycle dealer, Mark Webber gravitated towards four-wheeled competition as his father was not keen for him to take up bike racing. He served his apprenticeship in karts and Formula Ford in his native country before departing to try his hand in the bigger European arena.

Crash at Le Mans

Webber took 2nd place in the British Formula Ford championship in 1996, and 4th in the British F3 series the following year. He turned to sports cars in 1998, accepting an offer from Mercedes to compete in the FIA GT series. Partnering Bernd Schneider, who had won the inaugural championship the previous year, Webber took 2nd place, but his sports car career came to an abrupt end after a spectacular 180mph crash at Le Mans in 1999. He spent the next two years competing in the F3000 series, finishing in the top three on both occasions.

Graduating to F1

While competing in F3, Webber was also on the F1 fringe as a test driver, for Arrows in 2000 and Benetton in 2001. When Benetton morphed into Renault in 2002, Fernando Alonso was given the test driver berth, on the back of a good showing with Minardi, and Webber moved in the opposite direction. Compatriot Paul Stoddard had just taken over at Minardi, and he must have been delighted as Webber finished 5th on his F1 debut in Melbourne. It was Minardi's first points for three years; unfortunately, the rest of the season was a blank for Webber and the team.

There followed two seasons with the ailing Jaguar team, and 11 scoring races represented a decent return in the final throes before Red Bull took over the concern. Webber joined Williams in 2005 and had his best return to date, 36 points, six of those coming at Monaco, where he scored his first podium finish. After a disappointing 2006 – 10 retirements and a mere seven-point haul – Webber moved to Red Bull. He gained another podium at the 2007 European GP, but remained anchored in the midfield division of the Drivers' championship.

Acknowledgements

Thanks to everyone at LAT especially Peter Higham, Tim Wright,
Kevin Wood, Zoë Mayho and the digital team John Tingle,
Tim Clarke and Alastair Staley.

Thanks also to Vicki Harris, Frances Hill and John Dunne